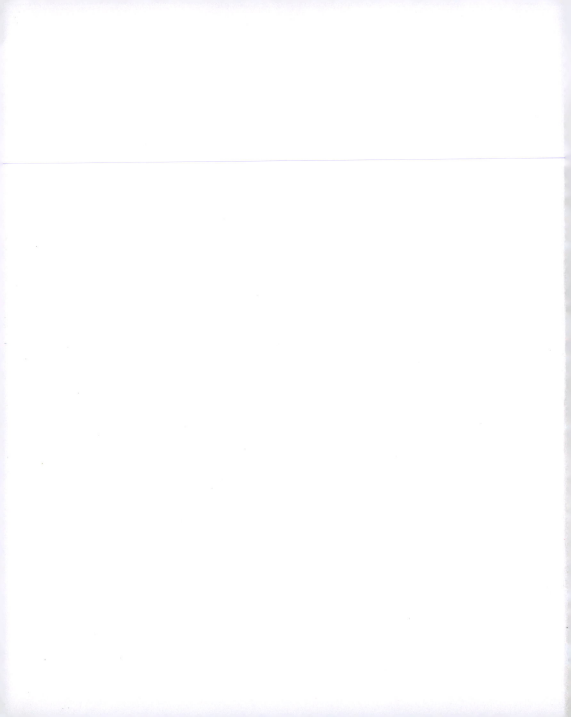

MADE IN THE OFFICE

Frances Lincoln Limited
A subsidiary of Quarto Publishing Group UK
74-77 White Lion Street
London N1 9PF

Made in the Office
Copyright © Frances Lincoln 2016
Text and photographs copyright © Rachel Maylor 2016
Design: Sarah Allberrey
Commissioning Editor: Zena Alkayat
Editor: Anna Watson

A catalogue record for this book is available from
the British Library.

ISBN 978-0-7112-3821-3

Printed and bound in China

9 8 7 6 5 4 3 2 1

Quarto is the authority on a wide range of topics.

Quarto educates, entertains and enriches the lives of
our readers – enthusiasts and lovers of hands-on living.

www.QuartoKnows.com

MADE IN THE OFFICE

TASTY & HASTY MEALS
WITH JUST A KETTLE,
TOASTER & MICROWAVE

 RACHEL MAYLOR

FRANCES
LINCOLN

Contents

BECOMING AN OFFICE COOK

The idea for this book came about a couple of months after I moved to London to start a new job. My daily meals had quickly come to consist of just a few depressing options, none of them particularly healthy, tasty or filling. Between the pressure of impressing in my new role and a full-on workload, my diet had suffered.

On my way into work I would often pick up a sugar-laden granola bar to curb the hunger that crept up during a long commute. By lunchtime I would be so ravenous I'd rush out of the office and grab the first thing I saw: usually a limp salad, takeaway soup or a dangerously salty (yet somehow still bland) sandwich. Then came the mid-afternoon slump. By three o'clock I'd be reaching for the biscuits as they made their way round the office, and would sometimes spend the rest of the working day grazing on yet more sugary snacks – treats brought in by a colleague, or a slice of day-old birthday cake. By the time I got home (still unsatisfied), all I wanted was a big, carby dinner. My breakfasts and lunches were boring, repetitive and beige, and provided me with little energy to see me through the day. I love cooking and eating, so it was disappointing that my workday meals were so drab.

It's a trap many of us fall into – eating healthily, quickly and conveniently isn't cheap, and working full-time can be all-consuming. I've never been keen on spending my precious evenings preparing my lunch in advance and leftovers rarely taste as good the next day, if they last at all! I knew there had to be a better way. I resolved to put my lunch hour to better use – though as it turned out, making wholesome breakfasts and lunches didn't take that long at all.

I started thinking about what I could make with the appliances in my office kitchen (just a kettle, a microwave and a toaster), as well as the handful of motley utensils. It initially seemed like a limiting selection, but there are plenty of foods you can cook just as well in a microwave as you can on a hob or in the oven - plus they take a fraction of the time!

Everything had to be quick to prepare and the ingredients easy to get hold of - things I could easily buy from a nearby supermarket or greengrocer. It also needed to be cheap - at the very least cheaper than buying pre-packaged meals each day. For inspiration, I thought about the meals I would make in the evening at home and how I could adapt them to the office kitchen.

It worked, really well. Preparing proper meals with varied, colourful and delicious ingredients was actually a fun thing to do each day, and suceeded in filling me up properly - no more reaching for the biscuit tin! I now look forward to my lunch and actually enjoy what I'm cooking and eating, rather than mindlessly consuming pre-packaged, salt- and sugar-loaded foods at my desk. I feel healthier, more awake and energised.

And the more I make, the easier, quicker and cheaper it becomes. As my colleagues looked on at my transformed lunchtimes in envy, I realised this neverending cycle of unsatisfying eating was a problem many people share and often moan about. So I decided to reveal my secrets. Here I've pulled together my favourite office recipes and office cooking hacks to help get you started on your journey to better eating at work. This is a book of inspiration to encourage you to enliven your breakfast, spice up your snacks and reclaim your lunch.

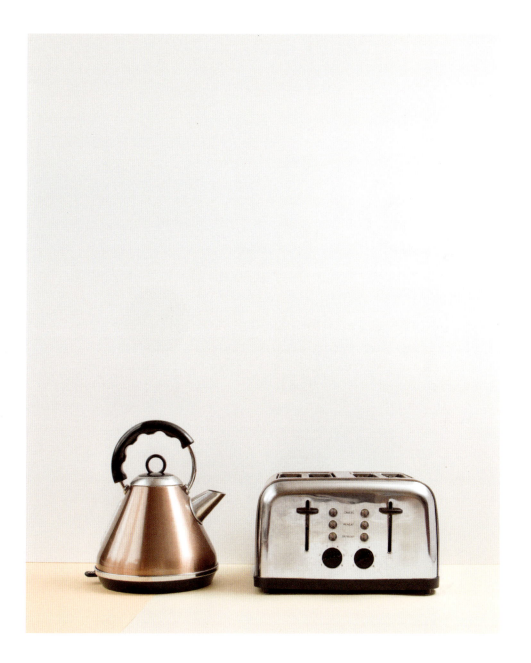

HOW THE BOOK WORKS

The aim of this book is to improve your meals at work so that they excite you more, sustain you for longer and cost you less. Preparing and enjoying appetising, well-balanced dishes doesn't need to take long and doesn't require expert culinary skills or any fuss the night before.

All of the ingredients in this book can be sourced from local supermarkets and I've used many of the same ingredients in multiple recipes (across breakfast, lunch and snacks) so you don't end up with half-empty packets.

That said, the recipes are a series of ideas intended to inspire your own experimentation with the ingredients you love. If you do opt to follow the recipes to the letter, you'll find dishes that are easy to prepare in the office kitchen. Some are light and fresh, while other options are more indulgent and filling. Take your pick, or mix and match.

The majority of the meals can be made on the day you want to eat them, and all of them using the cooking equipment in a basic office kitchen; there's no need to prepare anything at home or buy any obscure culinary tools. And none of the recipes take more than fifteen minutes to make, so you still have plenty of time to savour them before you get back to work.

Making an office lunch just a couple of days a week can dramatically improve your diet and many of the recipes will provide you with pre-prepared meals or leftover ingredients to last the rest of the week. Believe me, becoming an office cook couldn't be easier!

OFFICE CUPBOARD ESSENTIALS

Lurking at the back of my kitchen cupboards at home is a collection of exotic herbs, spices and special syrups I bought for one recipe and never used again: that's not what you want in the limited space you have in your office drawer or shared kitchen cupboard.

All of the essential ingredients listed below are intended to be used over and over again, so they won't sit gathering dust. And all of them are available from your local supermarket or greengrocer. Don't worry about going out and buying everything all at once, just pick them up as you go along and invest in the ingredients that make the biggest impact on your meal.

GRAINS Grains are extremely easy to prepare (see page 22) and are great for bulking out your meal and keeping you fuller for longer. Cous cous, quinoa and bulgur wheat are the most commonly used grains in this book, and all of them last for months when kept in a sealed container and stored in a dry cupboard.

OATS Warm or cold, oats are a wonderful way to begin your working day. I find chunky, whole-rolled oats are the most filling and they're particularly good at soaking up fruit juices (in a bircher muesli) and various milks. Keep them well sealed in a dry cupboard.

SEEDS AND NUTS These add a great crunch to breakfasts and salads, and can be enjoyed on their own as afternoon nibbles. Try to avoid paying over the odds at a supermarket and go to a health food store if you can. Many do good value bags or cut-price pick-and-mixes of broken nuts. Chia seeds can also be cheaper in health food stores.

DRIED NOODLES A good, solid base to a meal, and they quite literally keep for years. There are lots of varieties but some are easier to cook without a wok than others – rice noodles and wholewheat are generally best for softening quickly in hot water.

OLIVE OIL A staple at home, and equally valuable in the office kitchen; you may have half a bottle in the office kitchen already. Since you'll be adding it to salads and dressings (rather than cooking with it), it's better to have a good-quality extra virgin olive oil.

BALSAMIC VINEGAR/RED AND WHITE WINE VINEGAR Vinegars are an essential base to vinaigrettes and dressings, plus they store for ages. You'll also need a splash of vinegar (or sometimes lemon juice) when cooking salmon or chicken in the microwave.

HERBS AND SPICES I'm not suggesting you build up a spice rack, but a few well-chosen herbs and spices can transform simple dishes. Pots of paprika, cumin and cinnamon, as well as mixed herbs and fennel seeds, are readily available and can be used in both sweet and savoury dishes. A fresh basil or mint plant also doubles up as an attractive addition to your desk.

STOCK CUBES Vegetable stock cubes add extra flavour to grain-based dishes, and you can also use them when cooking meat and fish (see pages 21-22). Use about half a stock cube for every one mug of boiling water. Crush the cube at the bottom of the mug using the back of a fork, pour over the boiling water and mix until the cube is dissolved. You can then use in place of water when cooking grains or chicken.

SALT AND PEPPER Some sea salt and freshly ground pepper is a must. Both can be bought in ready-to-use mills that you can refill and keep on your desk.

LEMONS AND LIMES A squeeze of lemon or lime juice can liven up any dish. Use some as the base to a dressing or as a zesty garnish, and you might also need a squeeze of juice when you're cooking salmon, chicken and turkey. Pick up a couple of lemons or limes at the beginning of the week and save any leftover slices for a water infusion or fresh fruit tea (see pages 149-150).

GARLIC When stored in a dry cupboard, garlic can last for ages. A bulb is really cheap, but will add invaluable depth of flavour to dressings and sauces. Be careful not to overdo it though: raw garlic followed by a meeting with colleagues is not an ideal combination! Once chopped, crushed or grated, be sure to wash your hands with cold water – hot water seals the smell on to your fingers, which is not what you want for the rest of the afternoon.

SWEETENERS Maple syrup, honey and agave nectar can satisfy a sweet tooth, and all make for lovely toppings on porridge and other breakfasts. Don't go overboard though, as they're still high in sugar.

WASTE NOT WANT NOT

Many of us are guilty of throwing away and wasting too much food. The recipes in this book are designed to help you make the most of each and every ingredient. Throughout, I've added hints and tips for substitutions you can make to the suggested ingredients, and most of the recipes are designed to help you use up those last bits and pieces you've got in the cupboard or fridge.

Ingredients like salmon and chicken usually come in packets of two, or you might only need half a sweet potato or courgette at any one time. To avoid waste, a lot of the recipes use the same ingredients, and I've highlighted other dishes you can cook later in the week to use them up. In the meantime, store any leftovers in the fridge, alongside breads and fresh pasta (which keep for longer when chilled).

If you're lucky enough to have a freezer at work, take advantage. Meat and fish can keep for up to three months when frozen. Wrap each piece individually in cling film/plastic wrap or tin foil/aluminium foil and freeze immediately, always on the day of purchase. When you come to defrost, place the meat or fish (still wrapped) into a box or bowl (to reduce the risk of any juices leaking) and leave in the fridge overnight.

Fresh herbs can also be frozen and take no time at all to defrost. I'll often buy a bag of herbs but only use a few sprigs in a week. Don't throw them away - pop them into a sandwich bag and freeze them. When you come to use them again, just pluck off however much you want and run them under some lukewarm water, then chop or tear as you normally would. Same goes for fresh chillies.

EQUIPMENT & COOKING HACKS

Your office kitchen is probably better stocked than you realise. Alongside the usual plates, bowls, knives and forks you might find a chopping board, a vegetable peeler, a grater and maybe even a little colander or strainer. Below is a list of the equipment I find most useful. If a few bits are missing from your own office, there are plenty of high street shops that sell inexpensive versions of basic kitchen essentials.

MUG & KETTLE The humble mug is the most versatile (and most available) tool in the office kitchen. I use it in place of weight measures throughout the book. One mug in this book equals one everyday coffee cup in the US (not to be confused with the standardised 'cup' measure!). Kettles are ubiquitous in British office kitchens, but in the US you might need to use hot water dispensed from a Flavia or similar coffee-making machine.

PLASTIC POTS Every office has that one chaotic cupboard full of abandoned plastic boxes... it's time to put them to good use. They're brilliant for storing grains or noodles, as well as salads, fruit and leftover meat.

JAM JARS These are good for mixing up dressings: just pop everything in, seal with a lid and give it a good shake. I also use them for my overnight recipes (see pages 44-49) and as containers for noodle meals (page 116).

CLING FILM/PLASTIC WRAP An office cook's best friend. Use to cover any leftover ingredients for storage in the fridge, as a lid if you're using a mug to shake up dressings, and as a cover for bowls of food during the cooking process (both steaming and in the microwave). Check the box before buying to make sure it's microwave safe.

Cooking eggs, fish and meat in your office kitchen might seem like a lot of hassle, but it's actually very straightforward. These basic kitchen hacks can be applied to many of the recipes in this book, and once you've got the hang of them they can be used for your own culinary experimentation. Microwave timings may vary depending on model and age, so experiment until you find the time that's right for you.

COOKING EGGS For a poached egg, take a mug and fill it halfway up with cold water. Crack one egg into the water and let it sink to the bottom. Cover the mug with a plate or some cling film/plastic wrap and microwave on high for 60 seconds. While the egg cooks, fill a bowl with cold water. If after 60 seconds your egg isn't cooked, microwave for a further 15 seconds at a time. Once cooked, take the mug out of the microwave and carefully slip the egg into the cold water to stop it cooking any further. Scoop it up with a spoon and pop it on to a sheet of kitchen paper before transferring to your plate. For scrambled eggs, crack two eggs into a bowl and whisk with a fork. Add a knob of butter, a splash of milk and a sprinkle of salt and pepper. Microwave on high for 45 seconds. Break up the eggs with a fork to scramble, before cooking for a further 30 seconds. If the eggs are still runny, microwave for a further 15 seconds at a time.

COOKING SALMON I always thought that cooking fish in the microwave would leave the whole office smelling like a fishmongers, so I was pleased to find that it really didn't. It doesn't even make the microwave smell! Place a fillet of salmon into a shallow microwaveable dish, pour in enough cold water to reach halfway up the fillet and add two tablespoons of white wine vinegar. Cover with a plate or some cling film/plastic wrap and microwave on high for three minutes. Check to see if it is cooked - it should flake under pressure from a fork and appear light pink all the way through. If it isn't quite done, microwave on high for a further 30 seconds at a time.

COOKING CHICKEN AND TURKEY Chicken or turkey cooked in the microwave is both tender and moist. Place a chicken/turkey breast in a microwaveable bowl and cover with cold water. You can also add stock to the water if you like for extra flavour. Add a pinch of salt and pepper and a squeeze of lemon juice and then cover with a plate or cling film/plastic wrap. Microwave on high for three minutes. Once done, cut into the thickest part of the breast with a knife to check it is cooked - the flesh should be white throughout. If still pink, microwave for another 30 seconds at a time until cooked through.

COOKING GRAINS Adding quinoa, bulgur wheat or cous cous to your meal is a great way of introducing bulk and texture, and they all take just minutes to cook. First, boil the kettle. You will need one mug of boiling water per half a mug of quinoa or bulgur wheat, and around half a mug of boiling water per half a mug of cous cous. You can add stock to the water if you like. Using a sieve, rinse the grains in cold water to remove any starchy residue and then pour them into a microwaveable bowl. Next, pour the boiling water over the grain. Add a pinch of salt and pepper, cover with a plate or some cling film/ plastic wrap and microwave on high for six minutes. Once cooked, break up the grains with a fork - they should be light and fluffy.

MIXING A DRESSING The quickest and neatest way to make a dressing is to throw all of the ingredients into a jam jar or plastic box, seal the lid tight and give it a really good shake. It will also store in the fridge for 2-3 days.

FRESH FRUIT I often stock up on large fruit such as mangoes, pineapples and pomegranates for use throughout the week and store them in the fridge. I've found ways of using them in both sweet and savoury recipes so they're quite easy to get through.

QUICK STARTS

Bid farewell to sugary breakfast bars on your way into work and rushed bowls of cereal at your desk... this chapter contains straightforward and fuelling breakfast recipes that take no time at all to prepare.

warm nectarines with honey and lemon
and a seed and oat topping

time: under 5 minutes

2 ripe nectarines
1 tsp honey
a squeeze of lemon juice
2 heaped tbsp greek yoghurt
2 tsp chunky oats
mixed seeds

add toppings
dessicated coconut
flaked almonds
raspberries
cacao nibs
chia seeds

This is one of my favourite breakfasts – in fact, I would happily eat this at any time of day. You can swap nectarines for any other juicy fruit you want.

Slice the nectarines in half and remove the stones. Cut them again into quarters and place in a microwaveable bowl. Drizzle the honey on top, add a squeeze of lemon juice and mix with a spoon, making sure all the nectarine pieces are coated.

Microwave on high for 90 seconds, or until the nectarines have softened and warmed throughout. Remove from the microwave and give them another quick stir.

Add two big dollops of greek yoghurt and top with some chunky rolled oats and mixed seeds.

strawberry oat breakfast muffin

time: just over 5 minutes

¼ mug chunky rolled oats
2 tbsp wholewheat flour
2 tbsp buckwheat
¼ tsp cinnamon
½ tsp baking powder
a pinch of salt
¼ mug almond milk
½ mug strawberries
1 tsp maple syrup

In a mug, mix together the oats, flour, buckwheat and cinnamon. Add the baking powder and a pinch of salt. Pour the almond milk over the oat mixture and whisk it all together with a fork.

Remove the stems from the strawberries and cut them into small chunks. Add them to the oat mixture along with a teaspoon of maple syrup and stir them through.

Microwave on high for 90 seconds. If the mixture is still wet when you take it out, pop it back into the microwave for another 30-60 seconds. Once cooked, leave to stand for one minute.

Top with some strawberry chunks and eat straight from the mug.

sunny breakfast salsa

time: just over 5 minutes

½ small pineapple
½ ripe mango
a few mint leaves
1cm/⅓in piece of
    ginger, grated
a squeeze of lime juice
1 tsp honey or agave nectar
2 tbsp greek yoghurt

swap...
mango for honeydew melon
mint for basil

add toppings
sesame seeds
pumpkin seeds
pomegranate seeds

I'll often buy a fresh pineapple or mango on Monday morning and gradually use it up during the course of the week. Save any leftover fruit for a Tropical Chia Pot (page 44) or a Mango and Avocado Quinoa salad (page 76).

Using a sharp knife, cut your pineapple in half. Slice the skin off this section and discard. Chop the pineapple into segments around the hard core, so that it can be easily removed. Cut these segments into small chunks and tip them into a bowl, along with any leftover juices and pulp.

Next, cut the mango lengthways along one side of the stone. Taking the half without the stone, slice into the flesh length and widthways to create a checkerboard of small chunks. Slice just deep enough to create the pieces but be careful not to pierce the skin. Use a spoon to scoop out the mango chunks and tip them into the bowl along with the pineapple.

Next, finely dice your mint leaves and add them to the bowl along with the grated ginger. Squeeze in some lime juice, spoon over the honey and mix everything together.

Drop two big dollops of greek yoghurt on top and dig in.

toasted berry brioche

time: under 5 minutes

¼ mug cherries
¼ mug strawberries
¼ mug raspberries
1 tsp balsamic vinegar
1 tsp cinnamon, plus some
   to garnish
1 tsp honey or agave nectar
2 (or 3) slices of
   brioche bread

swap...
brioche for seeded or
   wholemeal bread

add toppings
1 heaped tbsp crème fraîche
   or yoghurt
a sprinkle of cacao powder

Sweet and satisfying, the warm brioche and bright red berries in this breakfast make it feel like a very fancy way to start the day. And it couldn't be easier to prepare. I recommend saving yourself an extra slice of brioche to mop up all those fruity juices.

Slice the cherries in half and discard the stones. Remove the stems from the strawberries and slice them into quarters. Tip them all into a microwaveable bowl along with the raspberries.

Add the balsamic vinegar, cinnamon and honey and mix everything together with a spoon. Microwave on high for 45 seconds.

While the berries cook, slice the brioche pieces and pop them into the toaster.

Check on the berries - they should be soft and warm. If not, put them back in the microwave for another 30 seconds.

Once golden, remove the brioche slices from the toaster and set aside on a plate.

When cooked, spoon the berries on to the brioche slices. Garnish with a sprinkle of cinnamon and eat while warm.

mashed banana and raspberries on toast

time: under 5 minutes

1 or 2 slices of seeded
  or wholemeal bread
1 large banana
a handful of raspberries
1 tsp honey
a pinch of cacao powder

add toppings
chopped dates or nuts
desiccated coconut

This breakfast reminds me of being a kid and I have it more often than I care to admit! Try it with some Raspberry and Chia Seed Jam (page 164) to make it extra special.

First, put the bread into the toaster. Next, peel the banana and chop it roughly into chunks. Tip the chunks into a bowl and gently mash with the back of a fork until soft and spreadable. In a separate bowl or mug, mash the raspberries.

When the toast is done, pop it on a plate and spread the banana mash generously on top. Drizzle with the honey, spoon on some of the crushed raspberries and garnish with a pinch of cacoa powder. Heavenly.

figs and ricotta on toast

time: under 5 minutes

1 or 2 slices of seeded
  or wholemeal bread
3 tbsp low fat ricotta cheese
½ tbsp honey
zest and juice of ½ lemon
1 tbsp chopped pistachios
2 fresh figs

add toppings
chopped dates or nuts
desiccated coconut

Another one of my favourite morning meals is this indulgent combination of creamy ricotta cheese and juicy figs – it's the cheese on toast of kings.

First, put the bread into the toaster. In a bowl or mug, mix together the ricotta cheese, honey and lemon juice, stirring until smooth.

Place the pistachos into a separate bowl or mug and gently crush them with the back of a spoon. Take the figs and thinly slice them lengthways.

When the toast is done, spread the ricotta cheese mixture on top and layer on the fig slices. Sprinkle with the pistachios and grate over the lemon zest to finish.

BIG BEGINNINGS

Fill up and get ready to face the day with these satisfying breakfasts. They're still quick and easy to prepare, but are scaled up to keep hunger at bay. Ideal if you've had an early start or morning workout.

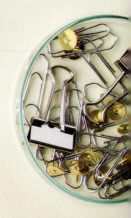

easy eggs florentine

time: just over 5 minutes

1 slice of seeded or
   wholemeal bread
2 large free range eggs
a small knob of butter
a handful of spinach
salt and pepper

swap...

spinach for chilli and lime
   guacamole (see page 57)

add

chilli flakes
chopped spring onion
cherry tomatoes

You don't have to wait for the weekend to get your poached egg fix – they're actually very easy to make at work. All you need is a mug, some boiling water and a microwave.

First, put the bread into the toaster.

Take two mugs (one per egg) and fill them halfway up with cold water. Crack the eggs into the mugs and let them sink to the bottom. Place a couple of small plates over the mugs, or cover them with cling film/plastic wrap, and put them in the microwave. Cook on a high heat for 90 seconds. If not done, microwave for a further 15 seconds at a time. While the eggs cook, fill a bowl or large mug with cold water.

When the eggs are done, take the mugs out of the microwave and transfer both the eggs into the mug of cold water. This will prevent them from cooking any further - you want those yolks nice and runny.

Spread the butter on to the toast and layer the spinach on top - this will wilt under the heat of the eggs. Use a spoon to scoop the eggs out of the water (tip the spoon ever so slightly over the bowl to get rid of any excess water) and pop them on top of the spinach. Season with salt and pepper.

chocolate orange porridge

time: just over 5 minutes

½ mug chunky rolled oats
1 mug milk
zest of 1 small orange
1-2 tsp raw cacao powder
a handful of raspberries,
    strawberries and blueberries
1 tsp goji berries (optional)
1 tbsp pumpkin seeds

swap...
pumpkin seeds for mixed seeds
    or chia seeds

add toppings
a couple of pieces of dark
    chocolate
a sliced banana

It feels naughty eating chocolate first thing in the morning, but it's a little more forgiveable if it's cacao powder. Made from raw cacao beans, it contains no refined sugars or dairy. And because it's raw, you don't need too much to get a really intense, chocolatey flavour.

Pour the oats and milk into a microwaveable bowl and mix together. Microwave on high for one minute.

Remove from the microwave and grate the zest of the orange into the bowl. Stir in the cacao powder and mix together well. Microwave for a further two minutes.

If the oats haven't completely absorbed the milk after three minutes, microwave for an additional 30-60 seconds. If the porridge is too dry, add a splash more milk to the bowl, stir and leave to settle for a minute.

Top with the fresh berries, goji berries and finally the pumpkin seeds for some added crunch.

creamy avocado and salmon bagel

time: just over 5 minutes

1 wholemeal bagel
½ avocado
½ lime
salt and pepper
3-4 slices of smoked salmon
1 tsp crème fraîche or yoghurt
2 chive stems, finely diced

swap...

the bagel for 2 slices of seeded
    or wholemeal bread
salmon for parma ham
chives for basil
avocado for cream cheese
    or ricotta cheese

add toppings

capers
chilli flakes

A smoked salmon breakfast bagel just cannot be beaten. Smoked salmon usually comes sliced in packets – use any leftover in a Salmon and Watercress Salad (page 106) for lunch later in the week.

Slice the bagel in half and put it into the toaster.

Scoop the flesh from half an avocado into a bowl. Mash with the back of a fork until soft and spreadable. Add a squeeze of lime juice and a pinch of salt and pepper and mix together.

Slice half of the smoked salmon into thin strips and fold them into the mashed avocado. Add the crème fraîche or yoghurt and mix again.

Take the bagel out of the toaster and spread one half with the avocado mixture. Layer the remaining salmon on top and garnish with the chives.

Add one more squeeze of lime, place the other half of the bagel on top and tuck in.

scrambled eggs on toast
with goats' cheese and herbs

time: about 5 minutes

1 slice of seeded or
   wholemeal bread
2 large free range eggs
a small knob of butter
a splash of milk
salt and pepper
2 chive stems
a few basil leaves
1 heaped tsp soft goats'
   cheese

swap...

basil and chives for parsley,
   thyme or dried mixed herbs
goats' cheese for feta cheese
seeded or wholemeal bread
   for sourdough bread

High in protein, eggs are an excellent way to begin your working day. In this recipe I've added some soft goats' cheese for a tangy twist on a breakfast favourite.

First, put the bread into the toaster.

Next, crack the eggs into a microwaveable bowl and whisk together with a fork. Add a knob of butter, a splash of milk and a pinch of salt and pepper. Whisk again and then pop the bowl into the microwave. Cook on a high heat for 45 seconds.

While the eggs cook, roughly chop, tear or snip the chive stems and tear the basil leaves into small pieces. Set aside.

Remove the bowl from the microwave and break up the eggs with a fork to scramble. Put the eggs back into the microwave for a further 30 seconds. By now, the eggs should be cooked but not dry. If the eggs are still runny, put them back into the microwave for a further 15 seconds at a time until done.

Once cooked, add a heaped teaspoon of crumbled goats' cheese to the eggs and stir it through.

Mix in half of the chopped herbs and spread the mixture on to the warm toast. Season with some salt and pepper and garnish with the remaining herbs.

tropical overnight chia pot

**time: just over 5 minutes
(plus overnight refrigeration)**

¼ mug chia seeds
¼ small pineapple
¼ ripe mango
½ mug coconut milk
1 tsp honey or agave nectar
coconut chips

swap...
mango and pineapple for
    raspberries and strawberries,
    pomegranate and orange or
    bluberries and peaches
coconut milk for almond milk
coconut chips for mixed seeds

This really is such an effortless breakfast. You can make it during your lunch hour or just before you leave at the end of the day – it'll be ready and waiting for you the next morning.

Pour the chia seeds into a jam jar or mug.

Using a sharp knife, cut a small section off your pineapple. Slice the skin off this section and discard. Chop the pineapple into segments around the hard core, so that it can be easily removed. Cut these segments into small chunks and tip them into the jar, along with any leftover juices and pulp.

Take your mango and slice off a small section. Cut into the flesh length and widthways to create a small checkerboard of chunks. Slice just deep enough to create the pieces but be careful not to pierce the skin. Use a spoon to scoop out the mango chunks and tip them into the jar along with the pineapple.

Next add the coconut milk and honey. Seal the jar with a lid, or tightly cover your mug with some cling film/plastic wrap, and give it a good shake to mix everything together.

Pop the jar into the fridge and leave to set overnight.

The next morning, tip the mixture into a bowl and top with some crunchy coconut chips.

fruity overnight oats

time: under 5 minutes (plus overnight refrigeration)

½ mug chunky rolled oats
½ tsp cinnamon
a handful of strawberries
a handful of raspberries
1 mug almond milk
1 tsp honey or agave nectar
1 tbsp pomegranate seeds

swap...

raspberries and strawberries
    for nectarines, peaches,
    blueberries or blackberries
almond milk for coconut milk
honey or agave syrup for
    maple syrup

add

cacao nibs
chopped almonds or pecan nuts

This is one of my favourite breakfasts of all time: it's tasty, filling and versatile. Here I've used red berries, but you can use any juicy fruit you want. The almond milk in this recipe gives the oats a wonderfully creamy texture.

Pour the oats into a jam jar or mug. Sprinkle the cinnamon on top and mix together.

Next, remove the stems from the strawberries and slice them into quarters. Put them in a bowl with the raspberries and gently crush the fruit with the back of a fork. Tip the pieces along with any leftover juice and pulp into the jar. Pour the almond milk over the mixture and then drizzle the honey on top.

Put the lid on the jar, or tightly cover your mug with some cling film/plastic wrap, and give it a good shake.

Pop the jar into the fridge and leave to soak overnight.

The next morning, pour the oats into a bowl. Sprinkle the pomegranate seeds and some extra berries on top and eat while still cold.

A quick tip: If you're using a fresh pomegranate rather than the pre-packaged seeds, roll it on a hard surface before cutting – this will release the seeds. Slice off a small section and use your fingers to turn it inside out and bash the seeds loose.

bircher muesli

time: under 5 minutes (plus overnight refrigeration)

½ mug chunky rolled oats
½ mug fresh orange juice
1 tsp dried apricots, chopped
1 tsp dried cranberries
a splash of almond milk
1 tbsp natural yoghurt
½ apple
1 tbsp blueberries
1 tbsp almonds

swap...
orange juice for apple juice
natural yoghurt for
    coconut yoghurt
blueberries for sliced pear
almonds for pistachios or
    hazelnuts

add
a teaspoon of maple syrup
    or honey
goji berries

Almost every supermarket or sandwich shop on the high street has their own version of the bircher muesli bowl, but they don't come cheap. It's just as easy to make your own as it is to pick one up on your way to work, plus it costs a lot less and is much lower in sugar.

Pour the oats into a jam jar or mug. Pour the orange juice over the oats and stir together.

Take your dried apricots and chop them into small pieces. Tip these into the jar along with the cranberries. Seal the jar with a lid or cling film/plastic wrap and refrigerate overnight.

The next morning, pour the oats into a bowl. Add a splash of almond milk and stir until the mixture has a porridge-like consistency. Next, drop a big spoonful of yoghurt on top.

Chop an apple in half and grate one half into your bowl. Finally, add a tablespoon of blueberries and a few almonds. Better than a pre-packaged pot any day.

A quick tip: squeeze some lemon juice over the other half of your apple to stop it turning brown. Store in the fridge for later use.

buckwheat and banana parfait

**time: just over 5 minutes
(plus overnight refrigeration
and soaking)**

⅓ mug buckwheat
1 mug cold water
1 banana
2 heaped tbsp chia seeds
⅓ mug almond milk
2 tbsp maple syrup
1 tsp cinnamon

swap...
almond milk for coconut milk
maple syrup for honey or
   agave nectar

add toppings
pecans
blueberries

Don't be fooled by the name – buckwheat is a gluten-free fruit seed and it's a great alternative to porridge oats. Brimming with nutrients and high in resistant fibres, it suppresses food cravings and helps lower cholesterol levels when eaten regularly. A true superfood.

Using a sieve, rinse the buckwheat in cold water to remove any starchy residue. Pour the buckwheat into a jar or mug and fill with cold water. Seal with a lid or some cling film/plastic wrap and set aside.

Peel the banana and chop it into chunks. Tip the chunks into a separate jar or mug along with the chia seeds and almond milk. Give the ingredients a quick stir and seal.

Put both in the fridge to soak overnight.

The next morning, remove the jars from the fridge. Using a sieve, rinse the buckwheat in cold water again - it may be quite slimy so wash until the water runs clear.

Pour the buckwheat into a bowl, add the maple syrup and stir through. Spoon the chia seeds and banana from the other jar into the buckwheat, add the cinnamon and mix it all together.

Drizzle over some extra maple syrup if you have a sweet tooth!

SUBSTANTIAL SNACKS

On those days when your stomach won't stop
rumbling, tuck into one of these healthy snacks.
They also make for great light lunches if you
have big plans for dinner.

beetroot and yoghurt salad

time: just over 5 minutes

2-3 large cooked beetroot
1 wholemeal pitta bread
1 heaped tbsp natural yoghurt
½ garlic clove, grated
1 tsp olive oil
1 tsp red wine vinegar
a squeeze of lemon juice
salt and pepper
a few mint leaves
a handful of rocket

swap...
mint for dill
rocket for spinach

add
spring onions
soft goats' cheese

Chunks of beetroot covered in fresh lemony yoghurt make for a colourful, flavour-filled snack, or a side salad to a piece of poached chicken (see page 22). Team with slices of toasted wholemeal pitta bread – they're perfect for mopping up that bright pink yoghurt dressing.

First, wash the beetroot to remove any excess juices (cooked beetroot often comes packaged in its own juices, or sometimes malt vinegar). Be careful when opening the packet - beetroot juice doesn't look good on a clean white shirt! Slice the beetroot into chunks and set aside.

Pop the pitta bread into the toaster.

Spoon the yoghurt into a bowl. Add the garlic, olive oil, red wine vinegar and lemon juice, mixing thoroughly as you add each ingredient so that the yoghurt doesn't split. Season with a pinch of salt and pepper and mix again.

Tip the washed beetroot into the bowl and coat it in the yoghurt mixture using your spoon.

Finely dice the mint leaves and stir them through before topping with a handful of rocket.

Take the pitta out of the toaster and cut into wedges.

guacamole bowl
with crunchy veg crudités

time: just over 5 minutes

1 avocado
¼ lime
½ small red chilli, sliced
sea salt and pepper
1 wholemeal pitta bread
3-4 cherry tomatoes
1 large carrot
⅓ cucumber
1 small pepper (bell pepper)

swap...
pitta bread for tortilla chips
carrots and cucumber for
   cauliflower florets

add
feta cheese
a few coriander (cilantro) leaves

Making guacamole is *really* easy and the fresh version tastes ten times better than the ready-made pots you'll find in the supermarket (those are usually pumped full of water and preservatives). This is also handily one of your five-a-day (at least!).

Take the avocado and slice it vertically in half. Remove the stone and scoop the avocado flesh into a bowl. Mash the flesh with the back of a fork until soft and spreadable. Add a squeeze of lime juice, a few of the chilli slices and a pinch of sea salt and pepper and mix it all together.

Put the pitta bread into the toaster.

Slice the cherry tomatoes into quarters, remove the seeds and add to the guacamole bowl, mixing well. Set aside.

Chop both ends off the carrot and cut it in half. Slice each half lengthways into quarters. Do the same with the portion of cucumber.

Cut into the top of the pepper around the stalk, removing the seed pod. Slice the pepper in half and then cut each half lengthways into thin wedges.

Take the pitta out of the toaster and cut into wedges.

Garnish the guacamole with the rest of the chilli slices, a wedge of lime and another pinch of sea salt and pepper. Get dipping.

tomato bruschetta
with an olive oil and chilli dressing

time: about 5 minutes

2 or 3 large vine-ripened
   tomatoes
¼ red chilli, sliced
¼ red onion, diced
2 tbsp olive oil
1 tbsp red wine vinegar
zest and juice of ¼ lemon
a chunky ciabatta roll or
   2 slices of stone-baked
   bread
1 garlic clove, peeled
a few basil leaves
sea salt and pepper

add
buffalo mozzarella
parmesan
grana padano

Anything on toast is a winner for me, but this dish is particularly appealing – especially come summer when tomatoes are at their most juicy and basil leaves are blooming. These bruschettas are a little taste of Italy in your office.

Slice the tomatoes into small chunks and tip them into a bowl along with the chilli and red onion. Add the olive oil, red wine vinegar and a squeeze of lemon juice and mix it all together. Set aside to soak.

Pop the bread into the toaster until golden brown. While the toast is still hot, rub the garlic clove on one side. You may need to be a bit rough with this step.

Tear up the basil leaves and mix them into the tomatoes. Spoon the mixture on to the garlic toast, add a pinch of salt and pepper and grate the lemon zest on top to finish.

A quick tip: when you wash your hands after rubbing in the garlic, use cold water and soap instead of hot water, as the heat acts to seal the garlic smell on your fingers. Squeezing a bit of lemon juice on your fingers helps too.

parma ham and soft cheese bites
with strawberries and balsamic vinegar

time: under 5 minutes

2 slices of sourdough bread
a handful of strawberries
1 tsp olive oil
1 tsp balsamic vinegar
salt and pepper
1-2 tbsp soft goats' cheese
3-4 slices of parma ham
a few basil leaves

swap...
goats' cheese for cottage cheese

add
a handful of rocket

Strawberries and basalmic vinegar are a match made in heaven, especially when laid on a bed of creamy goats' cheese and salty parma ham. Add any spare strawberries to your Fruity Overnight Oats (page 47) and use leftover parma ham for a Tomato and Mozzarella Salad (page 74).

Pop the bread into the toaster.

Cut the stems off the strawberries and slice them lengthways. Tip the strawberries into a bowl and add the oil, balsamic vinegar and pepper. Mix together.

Take the bread out of the toaster and spread the goats' cheese on top. Layer on the parma ham and top with the balsamic strawberry slices.

Tear some basil leaves and scatter them on top with a pinch of salt and pepper to finish.

green pea pesto and chorizo crostini

time: under 10 minutes

½ mug green peas
a chunky ciabatta roll or
    2 slices of stone-baked
    bread
1 tbsp of olive oil
sea salt and pepper
½ avocado
a few basil leaves
a few mint leaves
1 heaped tsp grated
    parmesan
2 radishes
1 garlic clove, peeled
3-4 slices of antipasto chorizo

swap...
chorizo for prosciutto

add
feta cheese

Fresh peas are often sold in small packets when in season. Though if you're lucky and have a freezer at work, you should buy a big bag of frozen peas to use again and again (this pea pesto is deliciously moreish).

Tip the peas into a bowl and boil the kettle. Cover the peas with the hot water and leave to blanch. This should take about three minutes for fresh peas and two minutes for frozen peas.

Put two to three slices of bread into the toaster.

When the peas are cooked, drain the water and add the olive oil and salt and pepper. Mash them gently with the back of a fork. Next, scoop the flesh from the avocado into the bowl with the peas. Mash again until the mixture is soft and spreadable.

Tear up the basil and mint leaves and drop them into the bowl. Sprinkle the parmesan on top and mix everything together. You can always add more cheese if you like.

Next, slice the radishes. Using a sharp knife, cut off the shoots and thinly slice the remaining flesh.

Take the bread from the toaster and rub one side with the garlic clove. Generously spread the pea pesto on top, layer over the chorizo slices and garnish with the radish.

A quick tip: when you wash your hands after rubbing in the garlic, use cold water and soap instead of hot water, as the heat acts to seal the garlic smell on your fingers.

warm balsamic tomatoes with prosciutto
on toasted sourdough

time: about 5 minutes

a big handful of
   cherry tomatoes
½ garlic clove, grated
1 tbsp balsamic vinegar
1 tbsp olive oil
salt and pepper
2 slices of sourdough bread
a few basil leaves
a handful of rocket
4 slices of proscuitto

swap...
prosciutto for parma ham
rocket for watercress

Cherry tomatoes roasted in balsamic vinegar are a summer staple of mine, and I've managed to recreate them using the office microwave. Soak up those warm juices with a couple of slices of toasted sourdough.

Slice the tomatoes in half and place in a microwaveable bowl.

Add the garlic, basalmic vinegar and olive oil to the bowl along with a pinch of salt and pepper and mix together.

Pop the bowl in the microwave and heat on high for 60 seconds. In the meantime, toast your sourdough slices.

Take the bowl out of the microwave. The tomatoes should be soft and hot. If not, microwave for a further 15-30 seconds.

Once the tomatoes are cooked, tear the basil leaves and add them to the mixture. Stir through.

Remove the sourdough slices from the toaster and top with the rocket, then lay the slices of proscuttio on top. Spoon the tomatoes on to the proscuttio to finish. And make sure to catch all of the delicous balsamic juices at the botton of the bowl!

chicken satay sticks

time: under 10 minutes

1 free range chicken breast
salt and pepper
juice of ½ lemon
⅓ cucumber
¼ red onion
1 tsp olive oil
1 tsp red wine vinegar
a handful of iceberg lettuce

for the satay sauce

1 tbsp peanut butter
1 tsp water
1 tbsp lime juice
1 tbsp soy sauce
1cm/⅓in piece of
 ginger, grated
a few coriander (cilantro) leaves

On first glance, this might seem like a complex dish to knock up in the office kitchen, but it's surprisingly simple. Chicken breasts poach to perfection in a microwave, while a humble jar of peanut butter provides a no-fuss base to a satay sauce. Save any leftover chicken for a Burrito Bowl (page 96) or Lemon and Mint Yoghurt Chicken (page 88).

Place the chicken breast in a microwaveable bowl and cover with water. Add a pinch of salt and pepper and a squeeze of lemon juice, and cover with a plate or some cling film/plastic wrap. Microwave on high for three minutes.

While the chicken cooks make the satay sauce. Mix the peanut butter, water, lime juice and soy sauce together before grating in the ginger. Give it a good stir and then tear up the coriander leaves and pop these in too.

Next, make the salad. Chop a third off a cucumber and cut it in half lengthways. Use a spoon to scoop out the seed centre. Cut the hollowed halves into slices and place in a bowl. Finely dice a quarter of a red onion and add to the bowl before drizzling with the olive oil, vinegar and a squeeze of lemon juice. Tear your iceberg lettuce leaves into shreds and add them to the mix. Use your hands to toss the salad together.

Take the chicken out of the microwave. Be careful as the bowl will be very hot. Check that the meat is cooked through – use a knife and fork to gently part the chicken in the middle. It should be white throughout. If it isn't, pop it back in the microwave for another 30 seconds at a time until done.

Once cooked, cut the chicken into chunks and slide them on to some wooden skewers (you can buy these at any good supermarket). Pop these on a plate and pour over the nutty satay sauce.

LIGHT LUNCHES

For a guilt-free midday meal that doesn't
compromise on flavour, try one of the
following lightweight lunch options.

feta and herb quinoa
with courgette and broad beans

time: about 10 minutes

½ mug quinoa

½ vegetable stock cube

3 mugs boiling water

salt and pepper

2 chive stems

a few coriander leaves

a few parsley leaves

1½ tbsp olive oil

2 tbsp green peas

2 tbsp broad (fava) beans

½ small courgette (zucchini)

1 heaped tbsp feta cheese

swap...

chives, basil and parsley for
    coriander (cilantro), thyme
    or any other combination
    of mixed herbs

courgette (zucchini) for avocado

feta cheese for cottage cheese

add

mixed nuts

Quinoa is a fantastic wheat-free alternative to grains such as rice and barley. Store in a cool, dry cupboard and enjoy again as part of a Mango and Avocado salad (page 76).

First, boil the kettle. Using a sieve, rinse the quinoa in cold water and then pour it into a microwaveable bowl. In a mug, crush half a stock cube with the back of a fork and fill with boiling water, stirring to dissolve the stock. Pour the stock into the bowl with the quinoa and add a pinch of salt and pepper. Cover with a plate and microwave on high for six minutes.

While the quinoa cooks, chop or tear the herbs and tip them into another mug. Pour over the olive oil and mix together.

Check on the quinoa. By now it should have absorbed over half of the water and some of the white centres of the quinoa should have separated. Give it a stir and then pop it back into the microwave and heat on high for two more minutes.

Next, put the peas and beans into a bowl and pour over two mugs of boiling water. Cover the bowl with a plate and leave to sit for three minutes. If you prefer them a little crunchy, blanch for just two minutes.

Chop the courgette into small chunks. Take the quinoa out of the microwave and check that it is soft and fluffy. If the grains are still a little tough, add a splash more boiling water and heat for one more minute at a time. Once cooked, pour over the herb oil and mix together.

Drain the peas and beans and add to them to the quinoa along with the courgette chunks. Crumble some feta cheese on top and sprinkle with a pinch of salt and pepper.

zesty courgette ribbons
with goats' cheese

time: just over 5 minutes

½ small garlic clove, grated
a squeeze of lemon juice
1 tsp olive oil
salt and pepper
1 large courgette (zucchini)
¼ tsp chilli flakes
1 handful of cherry tomatoes
1 heaped tbsp soft goats' cheese

swap...

goats' cheese for feta cheese
cherry tomatoes for
    sundried tomatoes

add

cooked king prawns (shrimp)
proscuitto
a couple of slices of crunchy
    ciabatta bread

Thin strips of courgette are a healthy alternative to pasta –
just add a burst of citrus and some creamy goats' cheese for
a taste of summer. Scale up by topping with some cooked
prawns or a poached chicken breast (see page 22).

In a bowl or mug, mix together the grated garlic, lemon juice and
olive oil. Add a pinch of salt and pepper and set aside.

Chop the ends off the courgette and using a vegetable peeler,
peel once or twice from top to bottom all the way around to
remove the skin. Discard this and then peel again on one side
from top to bottom to form long, thin ribbons of courgette. Keep
going to about midway through the courgette and then turn over
and repeat the steps on the other side of the courgette.

Place the courgette ribbons into the bowl with the lemon and
garlic oil. Sprinkle the chilli flakes on top.

Chop the cherry tomatoes in half and add them to the bowl.
Place a plate over the bowl and give it a shake to toss everything
together.

Lastly, crumble over the goats' cheese, add a pinch of salt and
pepper and tuck in.

tomato and mozzarella salad
with parma ham and basil vinaigrette

time: just over 5 minutes

a large handful of ripe cherry
    tomatoes or 3 large tomatoes
⅓ ball of mozzarella
2-3 slices of parma ham
a couple of slices of crunchy
    olive ciabatta bread

for the vinaigrette

a few basil leaves
2 tbsp olive oil
1 tbsp red wine vinegar
a squeeze of lemon juice
salt and pepper

swap...

parma ham for prosciutto
ciabatta for sourdough

My twist on this Mediterranean classic uses parma ham for a lunchtime protein hit. Pair with some olive ciabatta bread to catch every last drop of that delicous basil vinaigrette.

First make the vinaigrette - you will need a jar with a lid for this, or you can use a mug and cover it tightly with cling film/plastic wrap. Finely chop the basil leaves and place them in the jar. Add the oil, vinegar, lemon juice and a pinch of salt and pepper. Seal the jar with the lid and give it a good shake to mix all the ingredients together. Set aside.

Slice the tomatoes into halves (or smaller chunks if you're using large tomatoes). Place these in a bowl.

Pierce the mozzarella bag and drain the liquid. Take out the mozzarella and slice about one third off the ball (more if you really love mozzarella). Using your hands, tear this into small pieces and mix them into the bowl with the tomatoes.

Slice the parma ham lengthways in halves and weave around the mozzarella in the bowl.

Drizzle the vinaigrette over the salad and drop in a few extra fresh basil leaves. Pop your two slices of olive ciabatta bread on the side (you can always toast this if you like) and dig in.

mango and avocado quinoa
with a lime dressing

time: about 10 minutes

½ mug quinoa
½ vegetable stock cube
1 mug boiling water
salt and pepper
½ avocado
½ mango
a handful of cherry tomatoes,
    quartered
a few coriander (cilantro) leaves
½ lime
1 tbsp olive oil
1 heaped tsp soft goats' cheese

swap...

quinoa for cous cous
mango for cucumber
coriander (cilantro) for parsley
goats' cheese for feta cheese

This recipe is a midweek staple of mine, as it takes full advantage of mango and avocado halves I might have leftover from a Sunny Breakfast Salsa (page 28) or Guacamole Bowl (page 57).

First, boil the kettle. Using a sieve, rinse the quinoa in cold water and then pour it into a microwaveable bowl. In a mug, crush half a stock cube with the back of a fork and fill the mug with boiling water, stirring to dissolve the stock. Pour the stock into the bowl with the quinoa and add a pinch of salt and pepper. Cover with a plate and microwave on high for six minutes.

Meanwhile, slice the avocado vertically in half and gently twist the two halves apart. Taking the half without the stone, slice into the flesh length and widthways to create a checkerboard of small chunks. Slice just deep enough to create the pieces but be careful not to pierce the skin. Use a spoon to scoop out the chunks and tip them into a bowl. Next, take the mango and prepare in the same way as the avocado - slicing vertically in half around the stone, cutting into the flesh and then spooning out. Add to the bowl along with the cherry tomatoes.

Check on the quinoa. By now it should have absorbed over half of the water and some of the white centres of the quinoa should have separated. Give it a stir and then pop it back into the microwave and heat on high for two more minutes.

Once cooked, dice the coriander leaves and add them to the quinoa along with the lime juice, olive oil, avocado, mango and tomatoes.

Crumble the goats' cheese on top and add a pinch of salt and pepper to finish.

tabbouleh
with bulgur wheat and chickpeas

time: about 10 minutes

¼ mug bulgur wheat
½ vegetable stock cube
1 mug boiling water
salt and pepper
1 large bunch of parsley
1 large bunch of mint
a handful of cherry tomatoes,
    quartered
2 tbsp chickpeas
a squeeze of lemon juice
1 tbsp olive oil
2 tbsp pomegranate seeds
1 tbsp natural yoghurt

swap...
natural yoghurt for
    greek yoghurt

add
some falafel balls if you're
    feeling hungry!
cucumber
a dollop of hummus
toasted pitta bread

Canned chickpeas can be stored in the fridge for up to two days after opening – use any leftover chickpeas for the Spiced Bulgur Wheat Salad (page 109). If you have a freezer at work, freeze your herbs for future use, too – just run them under warm water to defrost.

First, boil the kettle. Using a sieve, rinse the bulgur wheat in cold water to remove any starchy residue and then pour it into a microwaveable bowl. In a mug, crush half a stock cube with the back of a fork and fill the mug with boiling water, stirring to dissolve the stock. Pour the stock into the bowl with the bulgur wheat and add a pinch of salt and pepper. Cover with a plate and microwave on high for four minutes.

Gather the mint and parsley into a large bunch and strip the leaves from the stalks. Dice the leaves and tip them into a bowl along with the tomatoes.

Take the bulgur wheat out of the microwave and give it a stir. Set aside for a couple of minutes.

Using a sieve, drain the chickpeas from their can and rinse them in cold water. Add two heaped tablespoons of chickpeas to the herbs and tomatoes and store the rest in the fridge in a plastic box.

Squeeze the lemon juice into the bowl and add the olive oil and a pinch of salt and pepper.

Drain any excess water from the bulgur wheat, add it to the bowl of herbs and tomatoes and mix everything together.

Garnish with the pomegranate seeds and a big dollop of yoghurt.

tuna and butterbean salad
with a lemon dressing

time: just over 5 minutes

3-4 tomatoes (use different
varieties to add extra flavour)
⅓ red onion
3 tbsp butterbeans
juice of ½ lemon
1 tsp of oregano
1 tbsp of olive oil
1 tbsp of red wine vinegar
1 can of dolphin-friendly
tuna in spring water

swap...
butterbeans for mixed beans

add
a few basil leaves
a slice of crunchy
ciabatta bread

Forget about those soggy sandwiches – tuna can be used in so many more exciting and delectable ways. Make sure to pick up a dolphin-friendly can!

Chop the tomatoes into chunks and add to a bowl.

Cut off one-third of an onion and slice it lengthways. Add to the bowl with the tomatoes.

Using a sieve, drain the butterbeans from their can and rinse them in cold water. Add three heaped tablespoons to the bowl of onions and tomatoes and mix together. Store the rest in the fridge in a plastic box and use for the Lemon and Mint Yoghurt Chicken on page 88.

Add a squeeze of lemon juice along with the oregano, olive oil and red wine vinegar. Stir through.

Open your can of tuna and drain the liquid. Spoon the tuna on to the butterbean salad. Squeeze some more lemon juice on top and season with a pinch of salt and pepper.

fig and goats' cheese salad

time: under 5 minutes

2 or 3 ripe figs

1 tsp honey

a large handful of mixed
    salad leaves

3-4 slices of prosciutto

1 tbsp pomegranate seeds

1 heaped tbsp soft goats' cheese

for the dressing

2 tsp balsamic vinegar

1 tsp olive oil

1 tsp honey

salt and pepper

add

lambs lettuce or watercress
    for some extra flavour

chopped walnuts

sliced pear

a slice of sourdough bread

The combination of sweet honey, rich cheese and juicy figs makes this dish feel downright decadent. Figs are at their best in late summer/early autumn, so make the most of them. Use any leftover goats' cheese for the Parma Ham and Soft Cheese Bites (page 60).

Slice the figs into quarters and place them in a bowl. Add one teaspoon of honey and toss the figs until they're coated all over.

Next, make the dressing. Pour the balsamic vinegar, olive oil and another teaspoon of honey into a mug and stir. Season with a pinch of salt and pepper.

Place the salad leaves on to a plate and layer the slices of prosciutto on top. Add the honeyed figs and scatter over the pomegranate seeds.

Pour over the dressing and crumble the goats' cheese on top.

A quick tip: If you're using a fresh pomegranate rather than the pre-packaged seeds, roll it on a hard surface before cutting – this will release the seeds. Slice off a small section and use your fingers to turn it inside out and bash the seeds loose.

fruity kale salad

**time: just over 5 minutes

2 large handfuls of kale
1 tsp olive oil
1 tsp red wine vinegar
pepper
½ avocado
½ mango
½ clementine
1 tbsp soft goats' cheese
1 tbsp pomegranate seeds
a handful of pistachios

swap...
avocado for beetroot
pistachios for almonds

High in fibre, low in fat and satisfyingly crunchy served raw, kale makes a great base for salads. Save the rest of the mango used here for breakfast tomorrow and make a delicious Sunny Breakfast Salsa (page 28).

Prepare the kale by first removing the tough stems. Use a sharp knife to slice off the leaves on either side.

Place the leaves in a bowl and drizzle with the olive oil and red wine vinegar. Use your hands to massage the kale, scrunching and releasing until soft. Season with a pinch of pepper.

Slice the avocado vertically in half and gently twist the two halves apart. Taking the half without the stone, slice into the flesh length and widthways to create a checkerboard of small chunks. Slice just deep enough to create the pieces but be careful not to pierce the skin. Use a spoon to scoop out the chunks and tip them into the bowl. Take the mango and prepare in the same way as the avocado - slicing vertically in half around the stone, cutting into the flesh and then spooning out into the bowl with the avocado.

Next, peel the clementine and rinse it under a cold tap, gently removing the white peel with your thumb. Slice the segments in half and add to the salad bowl.

Finally, crumble the goats' cheese on top and garnish with the pomegranate seeds, pistachios and another pinch of pepper.

A quick tip: If you're using a fresh pomegranate rather than the pre-packaged seeds, roll it on a hard surface before cutting - this will release the seeds. Slice off a small section and use your fingers to turn it inside out and bash the seeds loose.

FILLING LUNCHES

Perhaps you missed breakfast, or maybe you've
had a busy morning – sometimes you just need
food, and a lot of it. The recipes in this chapter
are designed to fill that void. Brimming with
protein and carbohydrate, they'll fuel you through
the rest of the afternoon and into the evening.

lemon and mint yoghurt chicken
on a bed of grains and butterbeans

time: just over 10 minutes

¼ mug bulgur wheat
½ vegetable stock cube
1 mug boiling water
salt and pepper
½ small courgette (zucchini)
¼ red onion
1 free range chicken breast
a squeeze of lemon juice
3 heaped tbsp butterbeans
a splash each of red wine
　vinegar and olive oil
a handful of salad leaves
　(rocket, spinach
　or watercress)

for the dressing

a few mint leaves
1 tbsp olive oil
a squeeze of lemon juice
salt and pepper
1 heaped tbsp natural yoghurt

Poaching chicken in the microwave is both quick and easy, honest! Team with butterbeans and bulgur wheat for a protein-packed start to your afternoon.

First, boil the kettle. Using a sieve, rinse the bulgur wheat in cold water and then pour it into a microwaveable bowl. In a mug, crush half a stock cube with the back of a fork and fill the mug with boiling water, stirring to dissolve. Pour the stock on to the bulgur wheat and add a pinch of salt and pepper. Cover with a plate and microwave on high for four minutes.

While the bulgur wheat cooks, prepare the dressing. Chop the mint leaves and pop them into a mug. Add the olive oil, lemon juice, salt and pepper and stir. Add the yoghurt and mix again.

Cut the courgette into chunks and finely dice the onion, and place them in a bowl. Take the bulgur wheat out of the microwave and give it a stir. Set aside for a couple of minutes.

Next, place the chicken in a microwaveable bowl. Cover with cold water, add a pinch of salt and pepper and a squeeze of lemon juice and then cover the bowl with a plate or some cling film/plastic wrap. Microwave on high for three minutes.

Using a sieve, drain the butterbeans from their can and rinse them in cold water. Add three heaped tablespoons to the onion and courgette mixture along with a splash of red wine vinegar and olive oil (store the rest in a plastic pot in the fridge). Drain any remaining water from the bulgur wheat and add it to the onion and courgette mixture. Stir and top with the salad leaves.

Now take the chicken out of the microwave. Be careful as the bowl will be very hot. Check that the meat is cooked – it should be white throughout. If not, microwave for another 30 seconds at a time until done. Once cooked, slice it into pieces. Leave it to cool for a minute or so and then layer it over the salad. Drizzle the yoghurt dressing on top and season with salt and pepper.

prawn and cous cous salad
with apple, courgette and sultanas

time: under 10 minutes

⅓ mug cous cous
¼ vegetable stock cube
½ mug boiling water
½ mug cooked king prawns
  (shrimp)
1 small courgette (zucchini)
½ apple
1 tbsp sultanas (golden
  raisins)

for the dressing

a few basil leaves
a few mint leaves
¼ small red chilli, finely diced
½ small garlic clove, grated
a squeeze of lime juice
1 tbsp olive oil

swap...

cous cous for bulgur wheat
apple for pear

add

mixed nuts

You can buy cooked king prawns either fresh or frozen. To defrost, run the prawns under a warm tap for a minute or two before adding to the cous cous mixture.

First, boil the kettle. Using a sieve, rinse the cous cous in cold water to remove any starchy residue and then pour it into a microwaveable bowl. In a mug, crush a quarter of a stock cube with the back of a fork and fill the mug halfway up with boiling water, stirring to dissolve the stock. Pour the stock into the bowl with the cous cous. Next, add the prawns and stir everything together. Season with some salt and pepper and cover the bowl with a plate or cling film/plastic wrap. Set aside.

In a separate bowl, make the dressing. Tear or chop the basil and mint leaves and add them to the bowl along with the chilli, garlic, lime juice and olive oil. Stir together.

At this point, check on the cous cous. Rake a fork through it - if it's soft, it's cooked. If not, add a bit more hot water, stir and then cover with the plate again. Set aside for another minute.

Chop the ends off the courgette, and using a vegetable peeler, peel once or twice from top to bottom all the way around to remove the skin. Discard this and then peel again on one side from top to bottom to form long, thin ribbons of courgette. Keep going to about midway through the courgette and then turn over and repeat the steps on the other side of the courgette.

Once it's ready, pour the dressing over the cous cous and stir through. Chop the apple into chunks and throw them into the cous cous along with the sultanas. Add the courgette and fold everything together.

A quick tip: squeeze some lemon juice over the other half of your apple to stop it turning brown. Store in the fridge for later use.

tuna niçoise
with poached egg and asparagus spears

time: under 10 minutes

3-4 small new potatoes
¼ mug cold water
3-4 cherry tomatoes
2 tbsp of mixed olives
a few leaves of iceberg lettuce
1 tbsp of olive oil
1 tbsp of red wine vinegar
juice of ½ lemon
½ tbsp of wholegrain mustard
½ can of dolphin-friendly
    tuna in spring water
4-5 asparagus spears
1 large free range egg

A true feast, this is one to sit back and savour. Have everything else ready before poaching the egg and asparagus tips, as these take very little time to cook and are best eaten straight away.

Chop the potatoes in half (or quarters if they're big) and place them in a microwaveable bowl. Measure one quarter of a mug of cold water and add this to the bowl along with a pinch of salt and pepper. Cover with a plate or cling film/plastic wrap and microwave on high for three minutes.

Next, slice the tomatoes and olives into halves and tear up some iceberg lettuce leaves. Place these in a separate bowl. Drizzle the olive oil, vinegar and lemon juice on top and add half a tablespoon of wholegrain mustard. Toss everything together.

Now boil the kettle for the asparagus tips. In the meantime, take the potatoes out of the microwave, drain the water and place them on a plate alongside the salad mix.

Open your can of tuna and drain the liquid. Spoon half of the tuna on to the plate and save the rest for another day.

Put the asparagus spears into a bowl and cover them with boiling water. They will take between one and two minutes to cook (the crunchier you like them, the less time you need to leave them to blanch).

For the poached egg, fill a mug halfway up with cold water. Crack the egg into the water and let it sink to the bottom. Place a small plate over the mug and microwave on high for 60 seconds.

Drain the asparagus spears and add them to the salad. When the egg is cooked, scoop it out of the water using a spoon (tip the spoon ever so slightly over the bowl to get rid of any excess water) and place it on top. Dig in immediately.

chilli poached salmon
with soy-lime noodles and broccoli

time: about 10 minutes

1 salmon fillet
a squeeze of lemon juice
1 tbsp honey
½ tsp chilli flakes
salt and pepper
2 tbsp white wine vinegar
1 nest of rice noodles
1 mug boiling water
a handful of tenderstem
  broccoli
¼ small chilli
a small chunk of carrot
a few coriander (cilantro) leaves

for the sauce

1cm/⅓in piece of ginger
½ tsp of sesame oil
juice of ¼ lime
1 tsp of soy sauce

swap...

tenderstem broccoli for
  sugar snap peas or
  edamame beans
rice noodles for wheat or
  soba noodles

Believe it or not, poaching salmon won't leave your whole office stinking of fish. Salmon fillets often come in packets of two, so use the other one for Salmon on Asian Slaw (page 99).

First, boil the kettle. Place the salmon in a shallow microwaveable dish and top with the lemon juice, honey, chilli flakes, salt and pepper. Use your fingers to rub the mix into the salmon. Add some cold water to the dish – just enough to reach halfway up the fish fillet. Add the white wine vinegar and cover with a plate or cling film/plastic wrap and microwave on high for three minutes.

Place a nest of noodles in a bowl. Measure out one mug of boiling water. Pour this over the noodles and set aside. The noodles will take two to three minutes to cook.

Next, cut the broccoli into small chunks and add them to the bowl of noodles and hot water. The broccoli should also take about two minutes, but if you like it softer, leave them to blanch for another minute or too.

While the noodles and broccoli cook, make the sauce. Grate the ginger into a jar or mug and add the sesame oil, lime juice and soy sauce. Seal the jar with a lid or tightly cover the mug with some cling film/plastic wrap and shake vigorously to mix.

Take the salmon out of the microwave and check to see that it has cooked through (see page 21). If not, microwave for another 30 seconds and check again.

Once cooked, drain the water from the noodles and broccoli and pour over the soy lime sauce. Give the bowl a shake to coat the noodles and veg and then place them on a plate.

When the salmon has cooked through, drain the water from the bowl and add to the plate. Garnish with a couple of slices of chilli, a small section of grated carrot and some coriander.

burrito bowl
with chicken, feta and sweetcorn

time: under 10 minutes

1 free range chicken breast
½ lime
salt and pepper
½ avocado
2 tbsp canned sweetcorn
2 tbsp black beans
½ tsp cumin
½ tsp cayenne pepper
a handful of cherry tomatoes
a few coriander (cilantro) leaves
1 tbsp of feta cheese
1 tbsp sour cream

swap...

avocado chunks for guacamole
    (see page 57)
black beans for pinto beans
feta cheese for grated
    cheddar cheese

add

a tortilla wrap

The burrito is a high street staple and very popular among my colleagues, but you can just as easily make your own for half the price. I've had a lot of fun experimenting with flavour combinations for this dish – you can add just about anything you want. Use the rest of your chicken for the Lemon and Mint Yoghurt Chicken (page 88).

Place the chicken breast in a microwaveable bowl and cover it with cold water. Add a squeeze of lime juice and a pinch of salt and pepper and then cover with a plate or some cling film/plastic wrap. Microwave on high for three minutes.

While the chicken is cooking, take your avocado half and cut into the flesh length and widthways to create a checkerboard of small chunks. Using a spoon, scoop the chunks out into a bowl. Add the sweetcorn to the bowl along with the avocado.

Take the chicken out of the microwave. Be careful as the bowl will be very hot. Check that the meat is cooked - it should be white throughout. If it's still pink, pop it back in the microwave for 30 seconds at a time until cooked. Once done, remove the chicken from the bowl and slice it into several strips. Leave to cool for a minute or so and then combine with the avocado.

Using a sieve, drain the black beans from their can and rinse them under cold water. Add two tablespoons to the chicken and avocado mixture and store the rest in the fridge in a plastic pot.

In a small bowl, mix the cumin and cayenne pepper and add the tomatoes, sliced into quarters. Microwave on high for 45 seconds. Once cooked, take the tomatoes out of the microwave and combine them with the chicken, avocado and beans.

Squeeze the lime juice into the bowl and sprinkle with some salt, pepper and the coriander leaves. Crumble the feta on top and add a big dollop of sour cream to finish.

salmon on asian slaw

time: 7 minutes

¼ small red cabbage
1 salmon fillet, uncooked
a squeeze of lime juice
salt and pepper
2 tbsp white wine vinegar
1 large carrot
½ apple
2 tbsp edamame beans
a sprinkle of sesame seeds

for the dressing

2cm/¾in piece of ginger
juice and zest of ½ lime
¼ small red chilli, diced
1 tsp sesame oil

swap...

red cabbage for white cabbage
seasame seeds for peanuts

This bright, fresh, zingy salad is full of flavour. Continue the Eastern theme later in the week and use up that extra salmon fillet with some Chilli Poached Salmon (page 94).

Make the dressing by grating the ginger and lime zest into a large bowl. Add the chilli and sesame oil and a squeeze of lime juice. Stir everything together and set aside.

Chop the tip off the red cabbage and take off the outer layer. Thinly slice the cabbage until you have a generous handful of strips and gently scrunch them to soften. Add these to the ginger dressing.

Place the salmon in a shallow microwaveable dish, add a squeeze of lime juice and sprinkle with some salt and pepper. Pour in enough cold water to reach halfway up the fish and add the white wine vinegar. Cover with a plate or some cling film/plastic wrap and microwave on high for three minutes.

Next, grate the carrot and apple into the bowl with the cabbage. Use your hands to toss the salad and set aside.

Take the salmon out of the microwave and check to see that it has cooked through (see page 21). If not, put it back in the microwave for 30 seconds and check again. Be careful not to overcook it as it will dry out.

Once cooked, add the salmon to the bowl with the slaw and top with the edamame beans and a sprinkling of sesame seeds.

A quick tip: squeeze some lemon juice over the other half of your apple to stop it turning brown. Store in the fridge for later use.

falafel and pomegranate pitta
with a seeded yoghurt dressing

time: just over 5 minutes

½ avocado

a squeeze of lime juice

salt and pepper

1 or 2 wholemeal pitta breads

4-5 falafel balls

2 tbsp pomegranate seeds

for the dressing

a few mint leaves

1 tbsp natural yoghurt

½ tsp olive oil

a pinch of poppy seeds

swap...

guacamole for hummus

add

cucumber and lemon to the
    yoghurt dressing to make
    tzatziki

grilled artichoke hearts

These pitta pockets will take you a matter of minutes to throw together. Falafel balls are quite tricky and time-consuming to rustle up from scratch, so I've cheated a little here and used the pre-made balls you can buy in packets from the supermarket. To make up for it, I've used my own mashed avocado accompaniment instead of shop-bought hummus. Perfect if you've got half an avocado leftover from earlier in the week.

Scoop the flesh from half an avocado into a bowl. Mash with the back of a fork until soft and spreadable. Add a squeeze of lime juice, a pinch of salt and pepper and mix it all together.

In a separate bowl make the dressing. Finely dice the mint leaves and mix them with the yoghurt, half a teaspoon of olive oil and a pinch of poppy seeds.

Put the pitta in the toaster.

Next, place the falafel balls on a microwaveable plate and heat on a medium setting for 45-60 seconds until warmed through.

Now take the pitta out of the toaster. Cut it in half and gently open the pockets. Spoon the guacamole and yoghurt mixtures into the pockets along with the pomegranate seeds. Crush the falafel balls and push them into the pittas with your fingers. Garnish with a few more pomegranate seeds and any leftover yoghurt.

A quick tip: If you're using a fresh pomegranate rather than the pre-packaged seeds, roll it on a hard surface before cutting – this will release the seeds. Slice off a small section and use your fingers to turn it inside out and bash the seeds loose.

sweet potato broccoli bowl
with tahini dressing and seeds

time: just under 10 minutes

1 small sweet potato
⅓ mug cold water
salt and pepper
a small handful of
  tenderstem broccoli
a small handful of
  sugar snap peas
2 heaped tbsp feta cheese
pumpkin seeds
1 tsp olive oil

for the dressing
2 tbsp tahini
juice of ½ lemon
2 tbsp water
½ small garlic clove, crushed
a pinch of salt
a few parsley leaves

swap...
feta cheese for soft goats' cheese
pumpkin seeds for pistachios

add
chicken or chorizo

First, boil the kettle for the broccoli.

Next, slice the sweet potato into chunks about two centimetres/¾ inches wide (discarding the gnarly ends) and place in a microwaveable bowl. Measure one third of a mug of cold water and add this to the bowl along with a pinch of salt and pepper. Microwave on high for 4 minutes.

While the potato cooks, cut the broccoli into chunks and add to another bowl along with the sugar snap peas. Take the kettle and pour in enough hot water to cover the veg. Leave to blanch for roughly two minutes. If you like your broccoli softer, leave for a little longer.

To make the dressing, add the tahini, lemon juice, water, crushed garlic and a pinch of salt to a bowl or mug and whisk until creamy. Finely dice the parsley, fold it into the mixture and set aside.

Take the sweet potato chunks out of the microwave and check to see if they're cooked. If they're still hard, put them back into the microwave for a further minute at a time until soft.

When the sweet potato is cooked through, remove from the microwave and drain off any excess water. Drain the water from the greens and add them to the sweet potato bowl. Pour over the tahini dressing and give the bowl a good shake so that all the veg is covered.

Finally, crumble the feta cheese on top and garnish with the pumpkin seeds, a pinch of salt and pepper and a generous drizzling of olive oil.

fresh tagliatelle
with lemon and parmesan cheese

time: about 5 minutes

1 large handful of fresh egg
  linguine or tagliatelle
salt and pepper
zest and juice of ½ lemon
1 tbsp olive oil
½ garlic clove, grated
1 heaped tsp grated parmesan
  cheese (plus extra for
  topping)
a small knob of butter
a few basil leaves

You can buy bags of fresh pasta from most supermarkets and it will keep in the fridge for later in the week – try using some for the Chorizo Linguine (page 115).

First, boil the kettle. Take a large handful of the pasta and place it in a bowl. Pour over the boiling water, add a pinch of salt and pepper and cover with a plate or cling film/plastic wrap. Set aside. It should take around two to three minutes to cook to al dente.

In a separate bowl, whisk together the lemon juice and olive oil. Add the garlic, parmesan cheese and a pinch of black pepper. Beat until the mixture turns thick and creamy.

Once the pasta is cooked, drain the water from the bowl and add the butter, stirring it through until it's completely melted. Tip the pasta into the bowl with the lemon dressing and mix it all together. Tear up some basil leaves and scatter them on top. Garnish with the lemon zest, parmesan cheese, salt and pepper.

prawn linguine
with basil vinaigrette

time: about 5 minutes

1 large handful of fresh egg
  linguine or tagliatelle
a few basil leaves
2 tbsp olive oil
1 tbsp red wine vinegar
a squeeze of lemon juice
a pinch of salt
½ mug cooked king prawns

If you're after a more substantial pasta dish, try this one with king prawns and a fresh basil vinaigrette.

Cook the pasta as per the instructions above. While the pasta cooks, prepare the vinaigrette. Rougly tear the basil leaves and pop them in a jar or mug. Pour over the olive oil, vinegar and lemon juice and add a pinch of salt. Seal the jar with a lid or some cling film/plastic wrap and shake vigorously to mix.

Drain the water from the pasta and place on a plate. Sit the prawns on top and douse with the vinaigrette.

smoked salmon and watercress salad
with new potatoes, gherkins and dill

time: just over 5 minutes

6-8 new potatoes
¼ mug cold water
salt and pepper
a sprig of dill
zest and juice of ¼ lemon
1 tsp of crème fraîche
3-4 gherkins
a handful of watercress
4 slices of smoked salmon

swap...

smoked salmon for smoked
   trout or smoked mackerel
crème fraîche for mayonnaise
watercress for spinach
   or rocket

add

capers

A plateful of protein and carbohydrate is just what you need if you're planning an evening workout. Use the rest of the salmon in a Creamy Avocado and Salmon Bagel for breakfast the next day (page 41) and the remaining potatoes in a Tuna Niçoise for another lunch (page 92).

Chop the potatoes in half (or quarters if they're big) and place them in a microwaveable bowl. Measure one quarter of a mug of cold water and add this to the bowl along with a pinch of salt and pepper. Cover with a plate or cling film/plastic wrap and microwave on high for three minutes.

Finely chop the dill and add it to a bowl along with the zest of the lemon and the crème fraîche. Mix together.

Take the potatoes out of the microwave and check to see if they're cooked. They should be hot and soft through.

Chop the ends off the gherkins and cut them into chunks. Toss them into the bowl with the potatoes, pour the dressing over the veg and give the bowl a shake to mix everything together.

Add a handful of watercress to a plate and layer the smoked salmon slices on top. Tip the potatoes on to the plate next to the salmon. Add a squeeze of lemon juice and a pinch of salt and pepper.

spiced bulgur wheat salad

time: just over 5 minutes

¼ mug bulgur wheat
½ vegetable stock cube
1 mug boiling water
salt and pepper
a handful of cherry tomatoes
2 tbsp roasted peppers
    (bell peppers) in oil
¼ red onion
a few coriander (cilantro) leaves
1 tbsp sultanas (golden raisins)

for the dressing
½ tsp ground cumin
a pinch of cayenne pepper
a pinch of cinnamon
a squeeze of lemon juice
1 tbsp olive oil
salt and pepper

swap...
coriander (cilantro) for mint
bulgur wheat for cous cous

add
feta cheese
chickpeas
courgette (zucchini) ribbons
orange zest

Keeping a handful of different spices in your office kitchen cupboard will transform your lunchtime experience. Here I use a warming combination of cumin, cayenne pepper and cinnamon to lift a super simple bulgur wheat salad.

First, boil the kettle. Using a sieve, rinse the bulgur wheat in cold water to remove any starchy residue and then pour it into a microwaveable bowl. In a mug, crush half a stock cube with the back of a fork and fill the mug with boiling water, stirring to dissolve the stock. Pour the stock into the bowl with the bulgur wheat and add a pinch of salt and pepper. Cover with a plate and microwave on high for four minutes.

While the bulgur wheat cooks, chop the tomatoes in half and add them to a bowl. Slice the roasted peppers and add these to the mix.

Next, make the dressing. Mix the spices together in a small mug and add the lemon juice, olive oil and a pinch of salt and pepper. Stir together with a spoon.

Take the bulgur wheat out of the microwave and leave to stand. In the meantime, dice the onion and add it to the dressing. Next take the coriander leaves and tear them into pieces.

Once the bulgur wheat has cooked, add the coriander to the bowl along with the sultanas and mix together. Pour over the dressing, throw in the tomatoes and peppers and give everything a good shake before serving on a plate.

turkey and pak choi noodle bowl
with a ginger soy sauce

time: under 10 minutes

1 free range turkey breast
a squeeze of lime juice
salt and pepper
1 nest of rice noodles
1 bulb of pak choi
2-3 small sweet peppers
  (bell peppers)
2 tbsp edamame beans

for the dressing

1 tsp soy sauce
½ tsp sesame oil
½ tsp rice wine vinegar
1 spring onion
½ small garlic clove
1cm/⅓in piece of ginger

swap...

rice wine vinegar for a splash
  of red wine vinegar or cider
  vinegar, but be careful not to
  add too much – they are
  sweeter and stronger than
  rice wine vinegar
turkey for chicken
pak choi for tenderstem broccoli

The crispy crunch of the pak choi in this recipe complements the moist turkey and melt-in-the-mouth rice noodles, and I've added a salty-sweet ginger soy sauce for good measure.

First, boil the kettle for the noodles.

To make the dressing, add the soy sauce, sesame oil and rice wine vinegar to a jar or mug. Chop the spring onions and tip these in too, then grate in the garlic and ginger. Place a lid on the jar or tightly seal the mug with some cling film/plastic wrap and give it a good shake. Set aside.

Take the turkey breast and place it in a microwaveable bowl. Cover the breast with water, add a squeeze of lime and a pinch of salt and pepper and then cover the bowl with plate or some cling film/plastic wrap. Microwave on high for three minutes.

As the turkey cooks, prepare the noodles. Place one nest in a bowl and cover with some boiling water. Set aside for two minutes.

Next, peel the leaves off the pak choi bulb and give them a good rinse under a cold tap. Add them to the noodle bowl to wilt in the hot water. Cut the peppers into slices and set aside.

Take the turkey out of the microwave and check to see it has cooked - the meat should be white throughout. If not, pop it back into the microwave for another 30 seconds at a time until done.

Drain the water from the noodles and pak choi and add the peppers and edamame beans. Slice the turkey pieces and layer these on top. Drizzle the dressing on top and there you have it - a texture and flavour sensation.

baked sweet potato
with tomato and paprika beans

time: about 10 minutes

1 medium sized sweet potato
4 tbsp tomato passata
1 tsp olive oil
a squeeze of lemon juice
½ small garlic clove, grated
1 tsp paprika
½ tsp cumin
½ can of mixed beans
a handful of spinach
1 heaped tbsp feta cheese
salt and pepper

swap...

sweet potato for a normal
    potato, although allow five
    more minutes in the
    microwave for this
feta cheese for soft goats' cheese
    or ricotta cheese

This is comfort food at its finest – just what you want on a cold, rainy day. You can top your baked potato with pretty much anything you like; here I've gone for an upmarket twist on the classic cheese and beans.

Trim off any gnarly ends of your sweet potato and then stab it all over with a fork. Wrap the potato in a dampened piece of kitchen towel and then cover in some cling film/plastic wrap. Place in a microwaveable bowl and microwave on high for five minutes.

While the potato cooks, make the sauce for the beans. Add the passata, olive oil, lemon juice, garlic, paprika and cumin to a bowl and mix everything together. Using a sieve, drain the beans from their can and rinse them in cold water. Tip half of the beans into the sauce and stir through. Store the rest in the fridge in a plastic pot.

When the time is up, take the potato out of the microwave and check to see that it is cooked. It should feel soft when you squeeze it (take care here as the potato will be very hot).

Next, cover the beans with a plate or cling film/plastic wrap and microwave on high for two minutes.

While the beans warm, place a handful of spinach on a plate. Unwrap the sweet potato, and slice it in half lengthways and place it on top of the leaves. The spinach will wilt under the heat of the potato.

When the beans are cooked (they should be hot through), give them a stir and then spoon on to the potato. Crumble your cheese on top, finish with some salt and pepper and enjoy while hot.

chorizo linguine
with fennel seeds and tomato sauce

time: just over 5 minutes

1 large handful of fresh egg
   linguine or tagliatelle
salt and pepper
½ small garlic clove, grated
½ tsp fennel seeds
a handful of cherry tomatoes
3 tbsp tomato passata
1 tsp olive oil, plus a little
   extra to garnish
a few coriander (cilantro) leaves
4-5 slices of chorizo (either
   ready-prepared antipasto
   slices or thin slices from
   a chorizo sausage)

swap...
chorizo for chicken
coriander (cilantro) for basil

add
fresh fennel
mozzarella

If you can find it and it's not too expensive, I recommend topping this dish with some fresh fennel – it adds a lovely crunch. If not don't worry, you'll still get that warm, aniseed flavour from the fennel seeds I've used here.

First, boil the kettle. Take a large handful of the pasta and place it in a bowl. Pour over the boiling water, add a pinch of salt and pepper and cover the bowl with a plate. Set aside. It should take around two to three minutes to cook to al dente.

Next, add the garlic and fennel seeds to a separate, microwaveable bowl. Crush the seeds with the back of a spoon. Chop the cherry tomatoes in half and add to the bowl along with the passata, a teaspoon of olive oil and a couple of the coriander leaves. Stir everything together.

Now slice the chorizo. If you're using antipasto slices, cut each slice lengthways into strips. If you're using chorizo sausage, then slice it finely. Add these to the bowl of passata with a pinch of salt and pepper, cover with a plate or cling film/plastic wrap and microwave on high for 90 seconds.

Once cooked, take the sauce out of the microwave and give it a good stir. It should be hot throughout.

Drain the water from the pasta and drizzle over some olive oil and a pinch of salt and pepper. Toss together. Finally, pour the sauce over the pasta and garnish with the remaining coriander leaves.

one-jar noodle soup

time: under 10 minutes

1 nest of dried noodles (I use
   wholemeal or soba noodles)
1 tsp miso paste
1 tbsp soy sauce
1 tsp tom yum paste (or
   ½ tsp thai red curry paste)
a squeeze of lime juice
a pinch of chilli flakes
a few drops of hot sauce
   (optional)
1 small bell pepper
½ carrot
a handful of red cabbage
1 spring onion
a handful of sugar snap peas
a handful of beansprouts
salt and pepper
½ vegetable stock cube
a few coriander (cilantro) leaves

add

any other vegetables you like!
cooked king prawns (shrimp) or
   chicken – add these to the jar
   just before you add the stock

This is a really flexible lunch method – you can use any vegetables you have to hand, so it's rarely the same twice. The staple ingredients are noodles and a stock cube, and everything cooks neatly in a jar.

First, boil the kettle - you will need enough water to fill the jar and to cover the nest of noodles in a separate bowl. Put the noodles in a bowl, pour over some boiling water and cover with a plate or cling film/plastic wrap. Set aside for two to three minutes to soften, or just one minute if you're using rice noodles.

While the noodles par-cook, take a mug and add the miso paste, soy sauce, tom yum paste and lime juice. Sprinkle in a few chilli flakes and stir everything together. If you like spice, add a few drops of hot sauce (I use Tabasco).

Drain the water from the noodles and tip them into a large jar. Pour over the miso paste.

Next, chop the pepper, carrot, cabbage and spring onions and add them to the jar, along with the sugar snap peas, beansprouts and a pinch of salt and pepper.

In a mug, crush the stock cube with the back of a fork and fill the mug with boiling water. Stir until the stock cube is dissolved. Pour the stock over the contents of the jar, making sure everything is covered. Top the jar up with some more boiling water if you need to.

Add a handful of coriander leaves, seal the jar and leave to stand for a couple of minutes. The stock will deepen in colour as it mixes with the paste. Open the jar, give it one last stir and slurp away!

a serious sandwich
with cheddar cheese and crunchy gherkins

time: under 5 minutes

1 ciabatta roll or 2 slices of
   sourdough bread
½ avocado
salt and pepper
4-5 slices of cheddar cheese
2 gherkins, sliced
3-4 slices of prosciutto or
   parma ham
2-3 sundried tomatoes
a few basil leaves

swap...
parma ham for prosciutto
cheddar cheese for soft
   goats' cheese

Sometimes there's just no substitute for a killer sandwich. A truly satisfying sarnie needs a variety of flavours and textures, all layered on a bed of fresh, crispy bread. This one is my own interpretation of the New York deli sandwich with parma ham, cheddar cheese and gherkins.

Slice the ciabatta roll in half, and pop it into the toaster. It only needs a minute or so to crisp a bit.

While the bread is in the toaster, make an avocado spread. Scoop the flesh from half an avocado into a bowl. Mash with the back of a fork until soft and spreadable. Add a pinch of salt and pepper and stir through.

When the bread is golden on the edges, take it out and spread the avocado on one half.

On the other half, layer up the fillings, starting with the cheese and the gherkins folowed by the parma ham, some sundried tomatoes and a few basil leaves. Drizzle with some oil from the jar of sundried tomatoes and then pop the avocado-slathered slice on top. A seriously good sandwich.

chicken and chorizo sandwich

time: under 5 minutes

1 free range chicken breast
1 ciabatta roll
1 tsp harissa paste
4-5 slices of chorizo
1 heaped tbsp feta cheese

First, poach your chicken breast (see page 22). While the chicken cooks, slice the ciabatta roll in half and pop it into the toaster. Once golden, take it out and spread with the harissa paste.

Once your chicken has cooked, cut the breast into slices and place them on the bread. Layer the chorizo pieces on top and crumble over the feta cheese.

summery salmon salad
with courgette ribbons, olives and pine nuts

time: about 5 minutes

a large handful of rocket
½ an avocado
1 large handful of mixed olives
2 tbsp pine nuts
a couple of radishes
1 courgette (zucchini)
1 tbsp olive oil
2 tbsp apple vinegar
3-4 slices of smoked salmon
salt and pepper

swap...
rocket for watercress
pine nuts for pistachios
salmon for cooked chicken
    (see page 22)

Use any leftover salmon from this recipe in a Creamy Avocado and Salmon Bagel (page 41) or in a Smoked Salmon and Watercress Salad (page 106).

Place the rocket in a deep bowl or on a large plate.

Take your avocado half and cut into the flesh length and widthways to create a checkerboard of small chunks. Using a spoon, scoop the chunks out into the bowl with the rocket.

Slice the olives in half and add to the salad along with the pine nuts. Next, slice the radishes. Using a sharp knife, cut off the shoots and thinly slice the remaining flesh. Add these to the bowl.

Chop the ends off the courgette and, using a vegetable peeler, peel once or twice from top to bottom all the way around to remove the skin. Discard the skin and then peel the courgette again on one side from top to bottom to form long, thin ribbons. Keep going to about midway through the courgette and then turn over and repeat the steps on the other side of the courgette.

Finally, mix the olive oil and apple vinegar in a small mug and drizzle it over the salad. Layer the salmon pieces on top and season with a pinch of salt and pepper.

smoked mackerel mix
with beans, peppers and avocado

time: about 5 minutes

4 heaped tbsp mixed beans

1 tbsp olive oil

juice of ½ lemon

salt and pepper

a few mint leaves

a pinch of chilli seeds or
    cayenne pepper

½ an avocado

2-3 small sweet peppers
    (bell peppers)

a large handful of salad leaves
    (lambs' lettuce or spinach)

1 fillet of smoked mackerel

swap...

mixed beans for chickpeas

mackerel for cooked
    herring, salmon or
    trout fillets

Mackerel fillets usually come in packets of three or four. Use the rest a couple of days after opening – I find mackerel goes particularly well with scrambled eggs on toast.

Using a sieve, drain the beans from their can and rinse them in cold water. Place four heaped teaspoons in a bowl along with the olive oil and a squeeze of lemon juice (store the rest of the beans in the fridge in a plastic pot). Add a pinch of salt and pepper and mix everything together.

Finely dice the mint leaves and add them to the beans. Lastly, take a pinch of chilli seeds or cayenne pepper and sprinkle on top. Set aside.

Now prepare the rest of the salad. Take your avocado half and cut into the flesh length and widthways to create a checkerboard of small chunks. Using a spoon, scoop the chunks out and add to the bowl with the beans. Next, slice the peppers and pop them into the bowl along with a large handful of salad leaves. Use your hands to mix everything together.

Tip the salad mixture on to a plate. Slice the mackerel fillet and layer it on top. Garnish with a squeeze of lemon juice.

SWEET TREATS

Everyone deserves a little treat now and
then, and for the sweet-toothed among
us, it's practically non-negotiable. Dip
into this chapter for some appealing
alternatives to that last stale biscuit.

cacao mousse
with banana, avocado and honey

time: under 5 minutes

1 ripe banana
½ ripe avocado
1 tbsp almond milk
2 tsp cacao powder
1 tsp honey
a handful of berries
    (blueberries, raspberries
    or strawberries)
a handful of almonds

swap...
berries for mango chunks
almonds for brazil nuts
almond milk for coconut milk

add
orange zest
coconut chips
diced mango

This is a wonderful little recipe for using up a leftover avocado half or soft banana sitting at the back of the fridge. They may look past their best, but they're just right for whipping up into a smooth dessert.

Peel the banana and chop it into chunks. Tip the chunks into a bowl and gently mash them with the back of a fork until smooth.

Using a spoon, scoop the avocado flesh into the bowl. Mash as before until smooth.

Pour in the almond milk and whip together. Next add the cacao powder and whip again.

Finally, drizzle in the honey, give it one last stir and top with the berries and a handful of almonds.

froyo fruit cups

time: under 5 minutes (plus 3 hours in the freezer)

6 tbsp natural yoghurt
1 tsp honey or maple syrup
a mix of soft fruit, such as:
   raspberries
   blackberries
   blueberries
   mango, diced
   nectarine, diced
   strawberries, halved

swap...
natural yoghurt for coconut
   yoghurt or any other
   flavoured yoghurt

add
a small dollop of chocolate
   spread (see page 163)

These are a cool treat on a hot day and will save you from reaching for sugar-loaded ice creams. Use the ice cube tray that comes with your freezer. If you don't have one, cupcake cases work just as well.

Fill each section of the ice cube tray about two-thirds of the way up with yoghurt. Drizzle a little bit of honey into each section and stir through. Place the fruit pieces on top of the yoghurt and freeze immediately. Leave for three hours.

Once frozen, taken the ice cube tray out of the freezer and run the back of the tray under some warm water for a few seconds – this will make it easier to remove the fruit cups. Take a plate and tip the ice cube tray upside down on to the plate, gently bashing the back of the tray to release the fruit cups.

Leave to soften on the plate for a couple of minutes and then pass around the office!

apple crackers
with almond butter and mashed berries

time: under 10 minutes

1 large apple
a sprinkle of cinnamon
1 tbsp raspberries
1 tbsp blueberries
2 tbsp almond butter

swap...
almond butter for peanut
    butter or cashew
    nut butter
raspberries and blueberries
    for sliced banana and
    strawberries

Dried apples are a brilliant way to scratch that 4pm sugar itch. Here I've topped them with some almond butter and crushed berries, but they're just as moreish on their own.

Cut the top and bottom off the apple and thinly slice it horizontally, removing the pips as you go.

Cover a large microwaveable plate with a piece of parchment paper (I find tracing paper works for this too!). Lay the apple slices on to the paper ensuring none of them overlap. Sprinkle with the cinnamon and then microwave on high for three minutes, or until the edges of the apple slices turn upwards.

While the apple cooks, tip the raspberries and blueberries into a bowl and gently mash with the back of a fork.

Once the apple slices have turned up at the edges, take them out of the microwave and turn them over. Pop them back into the microwave and heat on high for another 30 seconds.

Once cooked, take the apple slices out of the microwave and set them aside for two minutes. They will crisp as they dry out.

When the slices have crisped, pop them on to a plate and spoon a small amount of almond butter on to each slice. Top with the mashed berries and another pinch of cinnamon.

chocolate and banana rice cakes
with honey and cinnamon

time: under 5 minutes

1 large banana
1 tsp honey or maple syrup
2 plain rice cakes
a few pieces of dark chocolate
a sprinkle of cinnamon

swap...
rice cakes for oat cakes
chocolate for fresh berries

add
a thin layer of peanut butter

Rice cakes are a dream kitchen-cupboard staple because they last forever and can carry all sorts of toppings (both sweet and savoury).

Peel the banana and slice it into small chunks. Tip half of these into a bowl and gently mash them with the back of a fork until soft and spreadable. Spoon the honey into the mixture and mix it all together before spreading on to the rice cakes.

Top with the remaining banana slices and grate over some dark chocolate. Sprinkle with the cinnamon and tuck in.

blueberry and yoghurt rice cakes

time: about 2 minutes

a few mint leaves
1 tbsp greek yoghurt
zest of ¼ lemon
1 or 2 rice cakes
a handful of blueberries
1 tsp maple syrup

Tear up the mint leaves and add them to a bowl or mug with the yoghurt and lemon zest. Stir together and then spread the mixture on to your rice cake, topping with the blueberries. Lastly, drizzle over the maple syrup.

chocolate orange fondue
with fresh fruit pieces

time: just under 5 minutes

1 30g bar of good-quality
   dark chocolate
1 banana
a handful of strawberries
1 tbsp blueberries
1 tbsp blackberries
1 tbsp almonds
zest of ¼ orange

swap...
almonds for cashew nuts
   or walnuts
banana for apple, mango
   or pineapple

I like to think this strikes the right balance between healthy and indulgent. I've made a few suggestions for the fresh fruit pieces, but you can use pretty much anything you like.

Break the chocolate bar into small pieces and place in a microwaveable bowl. Microwave on high for 60 seconds.

While the chocolate melts, slice the banana and strawberries and add them to a plate along with the blueberries, blackberries and almonds.

Take the chocolate out of the microwave, give it a stir and heat again for a further 30 seconds. Once melted through, remove from the microwave and grate over the orange zest. Stir through.

This dish is best enjoyed while the chocolate is still warm – either dip the fruit into the chocolate or tip it all in and mix together.

almond and pear mug cake

time: just over 5 minutes

a small knob of butter
1 medium free-range egg
2 tsp caster/superfine sugar
1½ tbsp milk
4 tbsp plain flour
2 tbsp flaked almonds or
    chopped whole almonds
½ pear
1 tsp honey or maple syrup

Baking doesn't have to mean hours spent in the kitchen and countless different ingredients – this little cupcake rises in a matter of minutes, and it's sure to taste ten times better than that stale slice of day-old birthday cake.

First, melt the butter. Place a small knob in a mug and microwave on high for 30 seconds. Keep an eye on it as you don't want the butter to burn.

In a separate mug, lightly beat the egg and sugar together, before adding the milk, flour, melted butter and the flaked almonds. Whisk everything together with a fork.

Next, chop your pear in half and remove the seeds. Cut off the stalk and place your pear half in a microwaveable bowl with a splash of water. Cover with a plate or some cling film/plastic wrap and microwave on high for 45 seconds.

Once done, take the pear out of the microwave, drain the water and chop it into small chunks. Add these to the cake mixture along with the honey and stir through.

Place the mug into the microwave and heat on high for one minute. Give it a quick check when the minute is up – it should have risen quite a bit – and then pop it back into the microwave for another 30 seconds.

Once cooked, take the cake out of the microwave and leave to cool for one minute before diving in with your fork.

chocolate brownie mug cake

time: just over 5 minutes

4 tbsp plain flour
1 tsp caster/superfine sugar
1 tbsp cocoa or cacao powder
1½ tbsp milk
a small knob of butter
1 medium free-range egg
½ small banana
a couple of small cubes of
   dark chocolate
2 tsp of maple syrup

swap...
banana for strawberries
dark chocolate for
   white chocolate

add
chopped almonds or hazelnuts

You'll be the envy of the entire office when you pull this number out of the microwave. Gooey and moist, it's guaranteed to satisfy any mid-afternoon chocolate cravings.

In a large mug, mix together the flour, sugar and cocoa/cacao powder. Pour in the milk and whisk together with a fork.

In a separate mug, melt the butter. Place in the microwave and heat on high for about 30 seconds. Keep an eye on it as you don't want the butter to burn. Once melted, pour the butter into the chocolate mixture and stir through.

In the same mug you used to melt the butter, lightly beat the egg and then add it to the chocolate mixture. Whisk well.

Finely slice the banana and add the chunks to the mug along with the cubes of chocolate and maple syrup. Stir through.

Place the mug into the microwave and heat on high for one minute. Give it a quick check when the minute is up - it should have risen quite a bit - and then pop it back into the microwave for another 30 seconds.

Once cooked, take the cake out of the microwave and leave to cool for one minute before digging in.

SIMPLE DRINKS

Coffee is king first thing in the morning, but if you're looking to cut down on your caffeine intake or simply fancy a change, look no further. Here are a handful of different beverages ranging from summer coolers to winter warmers.

fresh mint and raspberry tea

a few mint leaves
a handful of raspberries

First, boil the kettle. Tear up the mint leaves and scrunch them tightly in your fist to release the oils. Drop them into a mug. Add the raspberries and gently crush them with the back of a fork. Pour over the boiling water and stir together.

warm mulled apple 'cider'

1 tsp maple syrup
a pinch of nutmeg
a pinch of cinnamon
zest of ¼ orange
1 mug cloudy apple juice

In a mug, mix together the maple syrup, nutmeg and cinnamon before grating in the orange zest. Pour the apple juice over the mix and pop into the microwave. Heat on high for 90 seconds.

warm cinnamon and honey milk

1 mug milk
½ tsp cinnamon
1 tsp honey

Pour the milk into a mug and microwave on high for 90 seconds.

In a separate mug, mix the cinnamon and honey together to form a paste. Pour the hot milk over the paste and stir until it has dissolved.

real hot chocolate

1 mug milk
½ 30g bar of good-quality
   dark chocolate
zest of ¼ orange

swap...
orange zest for chilli flakes
   or ground nutmeg

Pour the milk into a mug and microwave on high for 90 seconds.

Break the chocolate into small chunks and, once the milk is heated, add them to the mug. Grate in the orange zest and stir until the chocolate has completely melted.

Grate a little more chocolate on top and drink up.

blackberry and mint 'lemonade'

½ tsp agave nectar
zest and juice of ½ lemon
a handful of blackberries
a few mint leaves
chilled soda water
ice cubes

There's nothing like a cool glass of lemonade on a hot, sunny day. I've added some blackberries and mint leaves to this recipe for added flavour.

Add the agave nectar, lemon juice and lemon zest to a tall glass and stir together. Drop in the blackberries and gently crush them with a back of a spoon to release the juices.

Tear up the mint leaves and scrunch them tightly in your fist to release the oils. Add these to the glass and mix everything together. Pour over the soda water, add a couple of ice cubes and enjoy while cold.

mint ice tea

6 mugs boiling water
(if you're using a non-glass jug or bottle to infuse, use 1 mug cold to 5 mugs boiling water)
3 green tea teabags
2 tbsp honey (about 1 tsp per 1 mug boiling water)
a handful of mint leaves
a squeeze of lemon juice

I like to make a big bottle or jug of this in the morning to last me through the day. It's a cool alternative to a cup of tea on a warm day.

First, boil the kettle. Pour the hot water into a large jug or bottle. Add the teabags and leave to infuse for about ten minutes.

Take out the teabags and spoon in the honey. Stir until the honey has completely dissolved. Tear the mint leaves into pieces and squeeze them in your fist to release the oils. Drop them into the tea and leave it to cool before placing in the fridge.

Once cold, serve in a glass over ice with a squeeze of lemon juice.

refreshing water infusions

cucumber and mint
pineapple, orange and lemon
apple and cinnamon
lime and mint
strawberry and basil
lemon and lime
mango and raspberry
blueberry and mint

I have to actively remind myself to drink water at work. On busy days, I simply forget to refill my glass. But the experts are always telling us that hydration is key to a strong mental and physical performance, so I feel compelled to make sure I'm drinking enough water.

To prompt me to glug a bit more, I bought a large water bottle that I keep on my desk. Every morning I fill it to the top with water, and simply having it there reminds me to drink. For further encouragement, I started adding fruit to my bottle. These refreshing, preservative-free infusions infuse the water with flavour and colour and a bring a burst of freshness to my daily water intake – it makes it less of a chore and much more of a pleasure.

The combinations I've included on the previous page are tried and tested, but feel free to experiment with your own fresh ingredients. Simply slice up a handful of your chosen fruit (or lightly crush if you're using smaller fruit, such as berries) and add them to a large water bottle along with some herbs.

There are lots of water bottles on the market that come with baskets or compartments for this very purpose, but a standard plastic or glass bottle or jug will do. Fill the bottle with cool water and leave to infuse for five to ten minutes (or chill in the fridge) before drinking.

DRESSINGS & SPREADS

Sometimes a little dressing goes a long way. If you already have some lunch and it just needs a little extra zing, then whip up one of the following to drizzle on top. Or if you fancy something sweet mid-morning, try one of the delicious office-made spreads on toast or rice cakes.

honey and mustard dressing

1 tsp wholegrain mustard
1 tsp olive oil
1 tsp white/red wine vinegar
a squeeze of lemon juice

This dressing is a good alternative to the tahini dressing on the Sweet Potato and Broccoli Bowl (page 103). It keeps happily in the fridge for a couple of days.

Add all the ingredients to a jar or mug, seal with a lid or some cling film/plastic wrap and give it a good shake. That's all there is to it!

mint yoghurt dressing

2 heaped tbsp natural or
    greek yoghurt
a few mint leaves
1 tsp olive oil
a squeeze of lemon juice
salt and pepper

Add some diced cucumber to this recipe to make a refreshing tzatziki dip, or a pinch of paprika for some heat.

Add two heaped tablespoons of natural yoghurt to a bowl. Finely chop the mint leaves and add to the yoghurt. Mix them in along with the olive oil, lemon juice and a pinch of salt and pepper, stirring quickly so that the yoghurt doesn't split.

lemon and dill oil
with crumbled feta

a sprig of dill
juice of ½ lemon
1 tbsp olive oil
1 tsp red/white wine vinegar
salt and pepper
1 tbsp feta cheese

A zingy accompaniment to the Salmon and Watercress Salad (page 106).

Finely chop the dill and add to a jar or mug. Squeeze over the lemon juice, pour in the olive oil and vinegar and add a pinch of salt and pepper. Seal the jar with a lid, or tightly cover your mug with some cling film, and give it a good shake. Remove the lid and crumble the feta cheese on top.

ginger soy sauce

1 tsp soy sauce
1 tsp sesame oil
1 tsp rice wine vinegar
½ spring onion, chopped
1cm/⅓in piece of
   ginger, grated
½ small garlic clove, grated

The salty sweetness of this soy and ginger sauce adds depth to Asian-style dishes. Try with Chilli Poached Salmon (page 94) or Salmon on Asian Slaw (page 98).

Pour the soy sauce, sesame oil and rice wine vinegar into a jar or mug. Add the chopped onion and grated ginger and garlic. Seal the jar with a lid, or tightly cover your mug with some cling film, and give it a vigorous shake.

basil vinaigrette

a few basil leaves

2 tbsp olive oil

1 tbsp red wine vinegar

a squeeze of lemon juice

a pinch of salt

This vinaigrette is a great way to use up any basil leaves that are just past their best. It's delicious as part of a Prawn Linguine (page 104) or on a Tomato and Mozzarella Salad (page 74).

Rougly tear or chop the basil leaves and pop them in a jar or mug. Pour over the olive oil, vinegar, lemon juice and add a pinch of salt. Seal the jar with a lid or tightly cover your mug with cling film/plastic wrap and shake to mix.

pomegranate molasses vinaigrette

1½ tbsp pomegranate
    molasses

1 tsp mustard

1 tsp honey

1 tbsp red wine vinegar

2 tbsp olive oil

salt and pepper

Drizzle this vinaigrette on a Fruity Kale Salad (page 85) or over a Fig and Goats' Cheese Salad (page 82).

In a jar or mug, whisk together the pomegranate molasses, mustard, honey and vinegar. Seal the jar with a lid or tightly cover your mug with cling film/plastic wrap and shake well.

Take off the lid or cling film/plastic wrap and slowly whisk in the olive oil before finishing with a pinch of salt and pepper.

nutty chocolate spread

1 tbsp nut butter
1 tbsp cacao powder
a pinch of salt
1 tsp honey or agave nectar
2 tbsp almond milk

swap...
almond milk for coconut milk

A much healthier alternative to shop-bought spreads, this will keep for a week if sealed tightly and stored in a cool, dry place. Spread straight on toast for breakfast or use as a dip with fruit pieces for a sweet afternoon snack.

Spoon the nut butter into a jar along with the cacoa powder and a pinch of salt. Drizzle the honey on top and mix everything together with a spoon. Pour over the almond milk and whip until smooth and spreadable. Add more cacao powder if you like it rich.

coconut cottage cheese spread

2 heaped tbsp plain low fat
   cottage cheese
2 tsp desiccated coconut
1 tsp honey

I like to mix this spread with chunks of fresh nectarine and serve it on some toasted wholemeal bread as a light breakfast or afternoon snack.

In a bowl, whisk together the cottage cheese, coconut and honey into a smooth and creamy spread. Job done!

raspberry chia jam

2 handfuls of fresh raspberries
1 tsp chia seeds
1 tsp agave nectar or honey

Slather this jam on to warm toast with mashed bananas (page 33), or spoon on to some Apple Crackers for a mid-morning treat (page 130).

Tip the raspberries into a jar or bowl and mash gently with the back of a spoon until soft. Add the chia seeds and agave nectar and mix well. Pop the jam into the fridge and leave to set for about five minutes – this will allow the chia seeds to soften.

cream tea spread

a handful of strawberries
½ tsp honey
1 tbsp low fat cream cheese
a pinch of cinnamon

swap...
strawberries for raspberries
   or blackberries

Liven up your afternoon cuppa by pairing with some oat or rice cakes topped with some of this cream tea spread.

Cut the stems from the strawberries and slice them into chunks. Tip them into a bowl and gently mash with the back of a fork to form a chunky pulp. Add the honey and cinnamon and mix well.

Spoon the cream cheese into the bowl and stir into the strawberry pulp to form a creamy fruit spread.

Spread generously on to your carrier of choice and wash down with a nice warming cup of tea.

THANK YOUS

Thank you first to Robert for finding me and to Zena for taking a chance on me. Thank you to Anna for working on the words, Joanna for camera tips, and Sarah for the beautiful design. Thanks also to Diane, Cliff, Chris, Emma and Andrew for supporting me, and to Helen and Malcolm for patiently accommodating me. Thank you to Alison, Jennifer and Naomi for being encouraging at the beginning, and to Nathan for enduring me until the end. Finally, thank you to Haverstock for giving me a fantastic job and brilliant office to work and cook in.

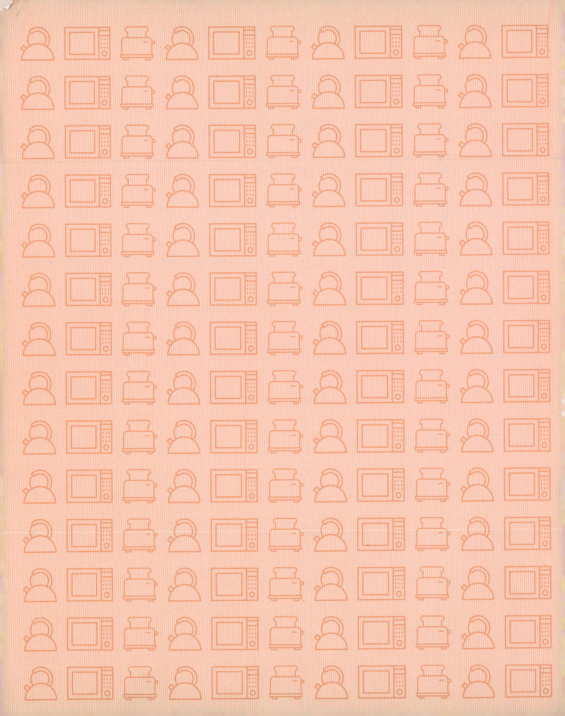